DATE DUE

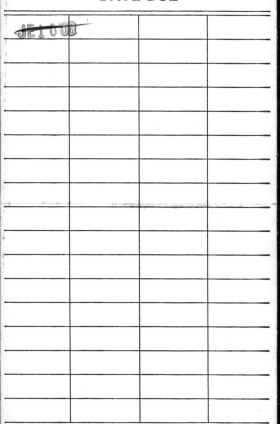

JE10'03			

DEMCO 38-296

THE NEW INFORMANTS

THE NEW INFORMANTS

The Betrayal of Confidentiality in Psychoanalysis and Psychotherapy

CHRISTOPHER BOLLAS AND
DAVID SUNDELSON

JASON ARONSON INC.
Northvale, New Jersey
London

Production Editor: Judith D. Cohen

This book was set in 12 pt. New Aster by Alpha Graphics of Pittsfield, New Hampshire, and printed and bound by Book-mart of North Bergen, New Jersey.

Library of Congress Cataloging-in-Publication Data

Bollas, Christopher
    The new informants : the betrayal of confidentiality in
psychoanalysis and psychotherapy / by Christopher Bollas and David
Sundelson
        p. cm.
    Includes bibliographical references and index.
    ISBN 1-56821-595-9
        1. Psychotherapist and patient—Moral and ethical aspects.
    2. Interpersonal communication—Moral and ethical aspects.
    3. Confidential communications—Physicians.   I. Sundelson, David,
    1946–   . II. Title.
    RC480.8.B65   1996
    616.89'023—dc20   95-14299

Manufactured in the United States of America. Jason Aronson Inc. offers books and cassettes. For information and catalog write to Jason Aronson Inc., 230 Livingston Street, Northvale, New Jersey 07647.

CONTENTS

ACKNOWLEDGMENTS

This book is the outcome of years of conversations with psychoanalysts and psychotherapists in the United States and, of late, in Europe. Without that evidence which derives from individual circumstances, and without the passionate support of those who have directly suffered from the erosion of a valued craft, this book would never have been written.

Even though we cannot individually thank the many, many people who have discussed the book with us over the years, we wish to do so to all of them and to indicate our gratitude.

We thank Murray M. Schwartz, Laurie Ryavec, Carol Morrison, and Jev and Sydnor Sykes for providing continuing forums for discussion of the topic.

We also thank Peter Wegner, who provided useful information on the situation in Germany, Jill Duncan, from the Institute of Psychoanalysis, and Marcy Schott at the Menninger Clinic. We are especially grateful for the meticulous research of Arne Jemstedt from Stockholm and for the kind assistance of Linda Mason in preparation of the manuscript.

We are grateful to Ed Corrigan, Pearl-Ellen Gordon, Jim MacKeith, and Gregorio Kohon for comments on the manuscript.

We reserve special mention for Colby Smith and for those psychotherapists and psychoanalysts like him who have refused to participate in the corruption of practice that operates under the name of "managed care." We appreciate his tireless assistance with our project.

Finally, we thank Lisa and Suzanne and our families for their encouragement and generosity.

INTRODUCTION

Why have psychoanalysis and the psychotherapies allowed the destruction of confidentiality between clinician and patient? At present we have a flood of disclosures from what was once a strictly private relationship: Nicole Simpson's therapist gives press interviews about her treatment; Anne Sexton's publishes transcripts of actual sessions; the psychiatrist who treated the Menendez brothers appears in court as a prosecution witness against his former patients. These are only the most celebrated instances. Some therapists may grumble about court orders to produce their clinical records, but most comply. Tens of thousands of others routinely report on their patients to scores of managed care providers.

Lawyers still have privileged relations with their clients, priests with their penitents, journalists with their sources, but therapists have allowed their privilege—equally if not more important to the practice of their profession—to be destroyed. With the mandatory reporting laws and managed care requirements, what patients say will now often be used against them. A pervert who seeks treatment because of pederastic inclinations may be reported to the police. A schizophrenic imagines his sexuality in persecutory ways and constructs a delusion of abusing someone; his therapist too may be legally obliged to report him. And then there is the child raised in a sexually oppressive environment who can only permit herself to imagine her sexuality by conjuring up a belief that she has been ritualistically violated. She will suffer horrific consequences when her therapist provides an account of these quite imaginary events to the authorities.

It seems almost inconceivable that psychotherapy—more dependent on privacy than any other profession—should have come to such a pass. Our book is an attempt to answer three related questions. How did the loss of privacy come about? What does it mean for clinical practice? What, if anything, can we do about it?

Chapter 1 examines the history of the psychotherapist–patient privilege: the principle that limits incursions by the legal system into a patient's privacy. Chapter 2 describes the rapid spread of the reporting laws and the blindness of the clinical professions to their meaning and consequences, while Chapter 4 attempts to explain these developments. Chapter 3 asks how the incursions on privilege have affected the clinical relation. Chapter 5 suggests courses of action in response to what we take to be nothing less than a crisis for the entire profession.

This book is written for psychoanalysts, psychotherapists, and other mental health practitioners, as well as for legislators, regulators, health industry personnel, and the general public. We believe that to explain why these incursions are so destructive, it is first necessary to explain something of what psychoanalysis is. This is not an easy task: the theory and practice of psychoanalysis is a vast topic. Nevertheless, we have tried to describe in readily understandable terms those central features of clinical work that cannot survive in the present climate.

Our study is also a call to arms for the profession. We know that some of the arguments we propose will be highly controversial. We believe that the developments we describe derive in large measure from the links between psychoanalysis and its parent professions: psychiatry, psychology and social work. These disciplines may not be capable of or interested in preserving the integrity of psychoanalysis. However, psychoanalysts have not yet declared their independence from disciplines that have to a considerable extent allied themselves with the forces of intrusion and disclosure.

It is too early to gain anything like a cool view of the present crisis. We are well aware that our analysis of the historical and cultural factors that converge to erode privacy in the mid-1990s is open to objection. We invite critical responses in the interest of developing a perspective that incorporates various points of view. We look forward to revising this small book as circumstances change and the issues are focused and refined.

In the course of writing it, however, we have already met with psychotherapists and psychoanalysts in more than half the United States. There is a profound confusion among even well-qualified clinicians about confidentiality and about the analyst's obligation to preserve privilege. We indicate various reasons for this confusion and suggest possible solutions, but we cannot adequately convey the fear and despair that now grip clinicians across the country. Europeans, South Americans, and Australians are not yet so anxious; their rights have not been undermined to the same extent. But we have found in consultation with clinicians from abroad a deepening sense of alarm over American developments. Indeed, the British Psycho-Analytical Society is sponsoring a one-day conference on confidentiality to take place in the autumn of 1995 in direct response to the concern of its members about the current situation.

Because they are so dramatic, it is more convenient to focus primarily on American developments although whenever possible we indicate parallel situations in England. We hope that an account of events in one place—especially in a book of this length—may illuminate issues that arise elsewhere in different form. About some things we feel certain. The response of psychoanalysts and psychotherapists to this crisis will have long-standing implications for the right of any person in any country to speak in private about his or her mental life.

1

BREACHING THE CONFESSIONAL

In a recent detective novel by the Israeli writer Batya Gur (1992), a psychoanalyst is murdered just before she is to deliver a lecture to her colleagues on "Ethical and Forensic Problems Involved in Analytic Treatment." The key to this murder, we learn, was the analyst's intention to disclose that one of those colleagues, a candidate for admission to the Psychoanalytic Institute, has been sexually involved with a patient—a patient who subsequently commits suicide. The murder also causes another crime. The analyst's medical records are stolen by one of her own patients, a prominent army officer. The officer fears that his career will be ruined if his superiors learn from publicity about the murder that he has been in treatment.

Gur's tale of a therapist's misdeed neatly presents both sides of the widespread current debate about confidentiality and psychotherapy. On one side are those who believe that a therapist must sometimes disclose confidential information to protect the innocent or punish the guilty. On the other is an equally strong belief that confidentiality is "at the core of the psychotherapeutic relationship" (Jagim et al., cited in Knapp and VandeCreek 1987, p. 10) and must be preserved to make that relationship possible.

The belief that disclosure may be necessary is embodied in the therapist's legal duty to give a warning about a patient's violent intentions. This is the so-called Tarasoff warning, derived from the celebrated case of *Tarasoff* v. *Regents of University of California* (1976) (17 Cal.3d 425). Tarasoff, a student at the University of California–Berkeley, was killed by another student who had been dating her and who had also been in psychotherapy at the student health center. Tarasoff's parents sued the university, alleging negligence in the failure to warn their daughter. The California Supreme Court held as follows: "When a therapist determines . . . that his patient presents a serious danger of violence to another, he incurs an obligation to use reasonable care to protect the intended victim against such danger. The discharge of this duty may require the therapist . . . to warn the intended victim or others likely to apprise the victim of the danger, to notify the police, or to take whatever other steps are reasonably necessary under the circumstances" (17 Cal.3d, p. 431). The therapist's legal duty is also embodied in the child abuse reporting laws that exist in all 50 states and that are the primary subject of this study. In Gur's novel, a therapist commits the misdeed whose disclosure—or threatened disclosure—causes a murder. This plot gives a twist to the usual reporting situation. Under the law, a therapist who learns from a patient about physical or sexual misconduct with a child, committed either by the patient or by some third party, must report that information to the authorities.

The contrary principle that patients need and have a right to confidentiality is as old as the Hippocratic Oath: "All that may come to my knowledge in the exercise of my profession . . . which ought not to be spread abroad I will keep secret and will never reveal." For psychotherapists of all kinds, the principle is axiomatic—although, as we shall see, there is surprisingly little reasoned support for it in the profession—and in law, it is embodied in the psychotherapist–patient privilege.

Fiction like Gur's is, if anything, less sensational than fact in staging the conflicting interplay of these beliefs. Consider a recent decision by the California Supreme Court in the case of two brothers, Erik and Lyle Menendez, charged with the shotgun murder of their wealthy parents.[1] Some time after the murder and under authority of a warrant, the

---

1. *Menendez* v. *Superior Court* (1992) 3 Cal. 4th 435.

Beverly Hills police seized three audiotape recordings during a search of the home and offices of Dr. Leon Jerome Oziel, a clinical psychologist who was Erik's and Lyle's psychotherapist. The cassettes contained an actual session Oziel conducted with both brothers as well as his notes of three other sessions.

Oziel invited the warrant party to listen to the tapes so they would understand that he had been threatened and, since the brothers were still at large, was in danger. After they were arrested, however, Oziel's position changed: he claimed that the psychotherapist–patient privilege applied to the recordings and that none of them could be introduced into evidence. The trial court rejected his claim, holding that the privilege did not apply. The California Supreme Court eventually sustained the trial court's ruling with respect to two of the sessions but reversed it with respect to the other two, including the actual session with Erik and Lyle. Defense attorneys for the brothers claimed that this part of the high court's ruling represented a victory for them. It is hard to know if they were right, since the first round of proceedings ended with a mistrial. (See also Goldstein 1990, for what is either the same case or a strikingly similar one.)

Like Gur's novel, the *Menendez* case has an atmosphere of mutual distrust and betrayal. Lyle and Erik may have consulted Oziel in the hope that he would portray them sympathetically if they were arrested and tried for murder. This was the view of the Court of Appeal, the intermediate appellate court that considered the issue of the tape recordings. On the other hand, Oziel's lover apparently overheard one therapy session with Lyle and Erik as an "eavesdropper." Oziel himself told the brothers that the recordings would be revealed if he were killed or if he disappeared mysteriously. He and his lover both testified at the evidentiary hearing regarding the tapes, and the Supreme Court quotes what it calls the trial court's "charitable" conclusion that each of them had "multiple motives, multiple motivations, multiple agendas."

The appearance of multiple agendas in a very different context contributed to the recent uproar over the publication of Diane Wood Middlebrook's (1991) biography of the poet Anne Sexton, who committed suicide in 1974. Middlebrook made extensive use of tape recordings of Sexton's sessions with a psychiatrist, Martin T. Orne. Dr. Orne not only provided Middlebrook with the recordings, apparently with the consent of Sexton's family, but he also contributed a foreward to the biography in which he explains his clinical reasons for making the tapes and his decision to release them to Middlebrook:

> When Professor Diane Middlebrook requested an interview to discuss my work with Anne, it was uppermost in my mind how important it had been to Anne always to try to help others, especially in their writing. Although I had many misgivings

about discussing any aspects of the therapy, which extended over eight years, I also realized that Anne herself would have wanted to share this process—much as she did in her poetry—so that other patients and therapists might learn from it. After much soul-searching, and after being assured that Anne's family had given their encouragement and approval, I allowed Professor Middlebrook to have access to the audiotapes and my therapy file, including the early unpublished poems Anne brought to therapy. It is in the spirit of helping others that I also offer here a view of what I believe contributed to Anne's untimely death. [Middlebrook 1991, p. xvii]

Orne goes on to criticize, not too indirectly, the other therapists who treated Sexton before she died.

Orne is not the first psychotherapist to find himself in such a controversy. A similar dispute arose over drawings that the late Jackson Pollock brought to sessions with his psychoanalyst, Dr. Joseph Henderson. After Pollock died, Henderson sold the drawings to a San Francisco art gallery, which exhibited them. The show was accompanied by commentary taken from an unpublished lecture by Henderson in which he used the drawings as a basis for psychological diagnosis of the artist. Pollock's widow, Lee Krasner, sued Henderson for violating Pollock's privacy by showing the drawings, but her suit was dismissed. In 1992, the drawings were exhibited once again (Cernuschi 1992, Frankenstein 1977).

Film stars seem to have fewer claims even than poets and artists to privacy in psychoanalysis. At a panel on "Issues in the Treatment of the Famous Patient" at the 1995 meetings of Division 39 (the division of psychoanalysis) of the American Psychological Association, two prominent members of the division presented papers on the treatments of Marilyn Monroe and Montgomery Clift by analysts who are no longer alive. The paper on Clift—or "Monty," as the analyst persisted in calling him— was accompanied by a large close-up photo of the actor's face, perhaps to substantiate the star-struck presenter's claims of its extraordinary beauty. The presentation focused not only on Clift's sexual proclivities but on those of his (at least formerly) respected analyst—all, of course, a cautionary tale to advance the audience's understanding of transference and countertransference dangers.

In all of these cases the conflict is the same: between the patient's (and, some have argued, the therapist's) right to confidentiality and to privacy, and some competing interest, whether that interest is called justice or art or biography or, as Orne puts it, "the spirit of helping others." In this book we want to define one version of the conflict. First, we will give a brief account of the psychotherapist–patient privilege, a rule created to protect the privacy of patients, focusing on some influential California decisions.

After that, we trace in somewhat greater detail the unusually rapid formulation and enactment of the child abuse reporting law. This law is an exception to the privilege, but unlike other exceptions, one that threatens to swallow the rule. We will again use California as a model and and will pay particular attention to the role of the mental health profession in the legislative history.

About thirty years ago a British psychoanalyst named Anne Hayman (1965) was subpoenaed to give evidence before the High Court about someone alleged to be a former patient. Hayman complied with the subpoena by appearing in court but refused to answer any questions about the alleged patient. She also prepared for a finding of contempt by arranging for a barrister to plead in mitigation of sentence, but her precaution proved unnecessary. "In the event," she wrote, "although my silence probably did constitute a contempt, the judge declared he would not sentence me, saying it was obviously a matter of conscience. In this he was acting within the discretion the Law allows him" (p. 785).

A few years later, a California psychoanalyst facing a similar situation was less fortunate. In December 1969, Dr. Joseph Lifschutz, a California psychiatrist, went to jail in San Mateo County for contempt of court after he refused for the second time to answer questions or produce records regarding his treatment of a former patient. Lifschutz spent only three days in custody (he was released while the California Supreme Court considered his appeal), but his case[2] is important. It illustrates clearly both the strengths and the limits of the psychotherapist–patient privilege in American law. It also shows the theoretical weakness in some of the positions held by those who, like Lifschutz himself, seek to defend the privilege.

A privilege, in the law, is an exception to the general rule that requires every person to testify in court. For a variety of reasons, the law recognizes certain relationships as special and therefore exempt from the requirement: those between attorney and client, priest and penitent, doctor and patient, journalist and source, husband and wife. Unlike some privileges, which have sources in common-law tradition (the law created by judges in England and the United States), the psychotherapist–patient privilege, in those states where it exists,[3] is entirely a creature of statute, that is, of legislative decision.[4]

---

2. *In re Lifschutz* (1970) 2 Cal.3d 415, 467 P.2d 557.

3. According to Knapp and VandeCreek (1987), 47 states and the District of Columbia have a privilege for psychologists, and 28 states have one for social workers. Psychiatrists are covered by specific statutes in 20 states and are covered under physician–patient privileges in 30 other states and the District of Columbia.

4. In California, the privilege is established by Section 1014 of the Evidence Code. The section provides in relevant part: "[A] patient has a privilege to refuse to disclose, and to prevent another from disclosing, a confidential communication between patient and psychotherapist if the privilege is

Although the related physician–patient privilege
has been heavily criticized by legal scholars and its
application severely limited,[5] the psychotherapist–
patient privilege, as the *Lifschutz* court acknowledged, "won legislative recognition in the face of
legal antipathy toward privileges generally."[6] In
California, the legislature concluded that "[a] broad
privilege should apply to both psychiatrists and
certified psychologists. Psychoanalysis and psychotherapy are dependent upon the fullest revelation
of the most intimate and embarrassing details of
the patient's life. . . . Unless a patient is assured that
such information can and will be held in utmost
confidence, he will be reluctant to make the full
disclosure upon which diagnosis and treatment

-----

claimed by (a) The holder of the privilege [that is, the patient,
his guardian, or his personal representative]. (b) A person
who is authorized to claim the privilege by the holder of the
privilege. (c) The person who was·the psychotherapist at the
time of the confidential communication, but such person
may not claim the privilege if there is no holder of the privilege in existence or if he or she is otherwise instructed by a
person authorized to permit disclosure."
5. See, e.g., Chafee (1943); 8 Wigmore, Evidence (McNaugh-
ton rev. 1961) section 2380a, at pp. 828–832 (all cited in the
Lifschutz opinion), and the long list of exceptions in California Evidence Code sections 996–1007. One commentator
concludes that the physician–patient privilege is "much
sound and fury signifying nothing" (Slovenko 1974, p. 650).
6. 2 Cal.3d at p. 434, n.20. Subsequent citations to the Lifschutz opinion are by parenthetical page references in the
text.

depends."[7] In one version or another, this sentiment echoes through California cases as a rationale for the protection that the privilege supplies.

And yet, Lifschutz did go to jail, and the California Supreme Court did sustain the conviction for contempt. How can this outcome be reconciled with what seems to be sympathetic endorsement of the privilege by both the legislature and the courts? The answer is that like most legal protections, this one is not absolute; the law also establishes various exceptions. The privilege may be limited when the patient voluntarily gives up his right to confidentiality, either explicitly or implicitly, when the therapist is appointed by a court to examine the patient, or where the legal issue is a deceased patient's intention concerning a will. Most reported cases about the privilege revolve around one or more of these exceptions, including *Lifschutz*.

The *Lifschutz* case grew out of a suit brought by Joseph F. Housek against John Arabian for damages resulting from an alleged assault. In addition to physical injuries, Housek claimed that the assault caused "severe mental and emotional distress." In a deposition, he stated that he had received psychiatric treatment from Lifschutz over a six-month period about ten years earlier. Arabian then tried to depose Lifschutz and to obtain all medical records relating to his treatment of Housek. Lifschutz ap-

---

7. Legislative Committee Comment to Evidence Code section 1014.

peared for the deposition but refused to produce records or answer any questions about the treatment; he even refused to state whether or not Housek had ever been his patient. After a series of proceedings, the Superior Court found him in contempt.

To justify his refusal to provide information, Lifschutz raised four different legal arguments, each of them significant. He argued that the order by the Superior Court violated (1) the constitutional privacy rights of his patients, (2) his personal constitutional right of privacy, (3) his right to practice his profession effectively, and (4) his right to equal protection of the laws (because clergymen could not be compelled to reveal confidential information in the same circumstances).

The court's response to this broad defense of the privilege was mixed. Justice Tobriner, the author of the opinion, describes psychotherapy as "a profession essential to the preservation of societal health and well-being" (p. 422). He recognizes that the patient "confides more utterly than anyone else in the world," and that "[i]t would be too much to expect [patients] to do so if they knew that all they say—and all that the psychiatrist learns from what they say—may be revealed to the whole world from a witness stand" (p. 431).[8] Relying on *Griswold* v.

---

8. Quoting *Taylor* v. *United States* (D.C.Cir. 1955) 222 F.2d 398, 401, which itself quotes from M. Guttmacher, et al., *Psychiatry and the Law* (1952).

Connecticut,[9] Tobriner concludes that there is protection in the United States Constitution for a patient's interest in retaining the "zone of privacy" (a concept from *Griswold*) that exists in a psychotherapist's office.

However, because of exceptions to the rule and the specific facts of the case, the court rejected each one of Lifschutz's arguments. The crux of the opinion is the court's response to the claim that the order to disclose violated the privacy rights of Lifschutz's patient. The court agrees that the statute gives Lifschutz the right to assert the privilege on his patient's behalf. However, Housek had already revealed that he had been in treatment. In addition, Housek did not claim the privilege when Lifschutz was ordered to testify. Applying the so-called patient-litigant exception,[10] the court concludes

---

9. *Griswold* v. *Connecticut* (1965) 381 U.S. 479. In this case, a landmark in the legal protection of privacy, the United States Supreme Court overturned as unconstitutional a Connecticut statute banning the sale of contraceptives to married couples.

10. The exception appears in Evidence Code sec. 912(a): "the right of any person to claim a privilege provided by Section . . . 1014 [psychotherapist–patient privilege] . . . is waived with respect to a communication protected by such privilege if any holder of the privilege, without coercion, has disclosed a significant part of the communication or has consented to such disclosure made by anyone." Evidence Code sec. 1016 applies the same principle to information concerning the "mental or emotional condition" of the patient.

that Housek had waived the privilege as to the in- ·
formation that he had been a patient.

The court's focus on the fact of waiver drama-
tizes a critical difference between legal and psychoanalytic ideas, a difference that Lifshutz and his
lawyers apparently failed to articulate. For a judge,
a waiver is binding on the person who gives it because that person is assumed to have acted freely
and autonomously. Psychoanalysis offers a different understanding of motive and action. Writing
about her experience in the case described above,
Anne Hayman (1965) gets right to the heart of the
matter. "Some of the United States have a law pro-
hibiting psychiatrists from giving evidence about
a patient without the patient's written permission,
but this honourable attempt to protect the patient
misses the essential point that he may not be aware
of unconscious motives impelling him to give permission" (p. 785).

Without this understanding that a patient's
waiver is not to be taken at face value, the California court had no way to reconsider the reasoning
that supports the patient-litigant exception. It could
express its respect for psychotherapy only by applying the exception narrowly, and this it did.

"Certainly," Tobriner writes, "in admitting the
existence of a psychotherapist–patient relationship,
plaintiff has not disclosed 'a significant part of the
communication' (Evid. Code, sec. 912) between
himself and Dr. Lifschutz so as to waive his right
subsequently to claim the privilege as to other ele-

ments of the communication" (p. 430). Tobriner
uses the case to limit the reach of the patient-litigant
exception, and he makes sure that it still leaves
substantial protection for the patient's privacy.
Thus he concludes that a court may compel disclosure only of those matters directly relevant to the
nature of the specific emotional or mental condition that the patient has voluntarily disclosed in his
lawsuit. "Disclosure cannot be compelled with respect to other aspects of the patient-litigant's personality even though they may, in some sense, be
'relevant' to the substantive issues of litigation"
(p. 435).

For Housek, this probably means that the actual
content of his treatment, ten years before the lawsuit, would remain privileged, even though the
opinion indicates that final determination would be
made by the trial court. To protect the patient's
privacy, the trial judge might make this determination after an *in camera* (in chambers) hearing,
out of the presence of opposing counsel and of the
jury. In that setting, the patient would have to reveal enough information to let the judge evaluate
his claim of irrelevancy to the issues of the lawsuit.
A patient or a therapist might disagree, but the
court believes that such disclosure "does not nec-
essarily entail an overbroad intrusion into the
patient's privacy" (p. 439).

When he turns to Lifschutz's claim of a personal
right of privacy, Tobriner's opinion reveals what
may be partly his failure to understand Lifschutz's

position and partly a weakness in the position itself. Lifschutz argued that because this right was
separate from that of any individual patient, he
could refuse to disclose confidential communications no matter what the patient wanted. Clearly,
Lifschutz derived this right from what he saw as a
duty not to Housek alone but to all his patients:

> At the contempt proceeding [Lifschutz's] attorney
> stated: [F]rankly, I am very pleased that the par-
> ticular patient, the plaintiff Housek, has taken no
> part in these proceedings because it presents the
> issue with perfect clarity. We are not on anyone's
> side here [in the underlying lawsuit]. We're just on
> the side of the doctor and medicine itself, because
> he is saying that no matter what the patient wants
> to do— . . . Now what I'm saying is that a doctor
> has an independent duty to all of his patients not
> to let any patient make him violate his oath that
> he has given to all patients at once. [p. 423, n. 4]

It seems equally clear that the court either failed
to grasp the notion of a duty owed collectively to
all patients or rejected it. The opinion refers initially
to "the psychological needs and expectations of
patients" (p. 423). However, patients as a group
then disappear from the analysis, replaced by
Housek, the particular patient who brought the
underlying suit: "[I]n the instant case the patient,
whose rights Dr. Lifschutz presumably seeks to
protect, is a party to the action, and had full opportunity to challenge the disclosures which have so

far been sought but declined to do so. Under these facts it would be inappropriate to find that Dr. Lifschutz could assert his patient's constitutional rights" (p. 423, n. 4).

Why did the court miss Lifschutz's central point? Perhaps because he failed to support it. There is no rationale for the duty Lifschutz identified, no explanation for his claim (which is only implied) that the disclosure of one patient's confidential communications causes damage to all of the therapist's other patients. The absence of such a rationale is fatal to the argument. Without it, the court simply abandons the idea of patients as a group. It rejects the notion of a right that exists independent of the patient-litigant who has waived his privacy by placing his mental condition at issue in a lawsuit:

> It is the depth and intimacy of the *patients'* revelations that give rise to the concern over compelled disclosure; the psychotherapist, though undoubtedly deeply involved in the communicative treatment, does not exert a significant privacy interest separate from his patient. We cannot accept petitioner's reliance on the *Griswold* decision as establishing broad constitutional privacy rights of psychotherapists. [p. 424]

This does not dispose of Lifschutz's arguments, however. He also argued that by compelling him to testify, the Evidence Code unconstitutionally impairs the practice of his profession. Justice

Tobriner identifies two different legal contentions underlying this claim: first, that the impairment of psychotherapy is so severe as to constitute an unconstitutional "taking" of a valuable property right—the doctor's right to practice; and second, "that compelled disclosure of any psychotherapeutic communication renders the continued practice of psychotherapy impossible and thus unconstitutionally constricts the realm of available medical treatment" (p. 425).

The first contention falls easily to what constitutional lawyers call "deference" analysis. On principle, courts "defer" to the will of the legislature in such areas as business regulation so long as the regulation is not too burdensome and there is some "legitimate governmental interest" to justify it. Here, that interest is a strong one that judges understand very well: "the ascertainment of truth and the just resolution of legal claims" (p. 425). The court's job is to weigh this interest against the psychotherapist's need for confidentiality.

As the opinion notes, the therapist's need, unlike those of the legal system, "exemplifies the type of question to which the judiciary brings little expertise" (p. 427). The court's lack of expertise appears again and again in the vagueness and uncertainty of its analysis: "[W]e doubt that the disclosure . . . goes so far as to constitute the claimed unconstitutional deprivation of that right. . . . all compelled disclosures may interfere to some extent with an individual's performance of his work"

(p. 425); "We do not know, of course, to what extent patients are deterred from seeking psychotherapeutic treatment. . . . [w]e can only surmise that an understanding of the limits of [the patient-litigant exception] may provide a measure of reassurance to the prospective patient" (p. 427).

The failure to educate the court, to provide a persuasive account of what takes place in therapy and what part confidentiality plays in the process, sinks Lifschutz's position. Where the judges are so uncertain about one of the competing interests and so familiar with the other, the outcome is a foregone conclusion: the court finds it easy to decide that the state's need for evidence is greater than the therapist's need for confidentiality. Similarly, where Lifschutz asserts that the erosion of confidentiality will inhibit patients "from participating fully in the psychotherapeutic process" (p. 426), uncertainty about what that process is and how it works fuels the court's skepticism: "[W]e cannot blind ourselves to the fact that the practice of psychotherapy has grown, indeed flourished, in an environment of a non-absolute privilege" (p. 426).

However, skepticism is not at the heart of the reasoning. Tobriner relies instead on the "limited nature of the intrusion into psychotherapeutic privacy actually at issue in this case" (p. 427)—on limits, that is, which his own opinion has defined. He emphasizes that the patient-litigant exception to the privilege has a kind of built-in compensatory mechanism. Even if it does deter some patients from seeking treatment, as Lifschutz claims, it should at the same time reassure patients that they are in control. They can choose to preserve the privilege that shields their privacy; they need only refrain from placing their mental condition at issue in litigation.

The last of Lifschutz's contentions is that the requirement of disclosure deprives him of equal protection under the Fourteenth Amendment because a clergyman would be protected where a therapist is not. The court applies a traditional "rational basis" approach to the problem. That is, he asks whether the legislature acted irrationally in creating the distinction. His conclusion is that where "toleration of religion exists by law, and where a substantial part of the community professes a religion practising a confessional system" (p. 428), it did not:

> Although in some circumstances clergymen and psychotherapists perform similar functions and serve similar needs, fundamental and significant differences remain. While many psychotherapists are no doubt strongly committed to the "tenets" of their profession, as indeed Dr. Lifschutz has exhibited by his determined action in the instant proceeding, the source of this commitment can be reasonably distinguished from the distinctive religious conviction out of which the penitential privilege flows. [p. 429]

It is interesting that in a footnote, the opinion cites the "Principles of Medical Ethics" of the

American Medical Association, noting the provision that a physician may not reveal confidences entrusted to him "unless he is required to do so by law" (p. 429, n. 9). As in the court's apparent failure to comprehend the notion of a duty owed not to one patient but to all patients, the weakness of the rationale underlying Lifschutz's position has allowed the court to reject it. Perhaps, if the psychotherapeutic community had a clearer "tenet" regarding confidentiality and could clearly explain the need for it, the equal protection argument might have prevailed.

Twenty years after *Lifschutz*, Justice Stanley Mosk, who concurred in *Lifschutz*, wrote the opinion in *Menendez*. This time, the issue of confidentiality arose in a criminal, not a civil, context, and the court dealt with the "dangerous patient" exception,[11] with an additional glance at the "crime or tort" exception.[12] Once again, we can see that the privilege

---

11. Evidence Code sec. 1024, which provides: "There is no privilege . . . if the psychotherapist has reasonable cause to believe that the patient is in such mental or emotional condition as to be dangerous to himself or to the person or property of another and that disclosure of the communication is necessary to prevent the threatened danger."

12. Evidence Code sec. 1018 which provides: "There is no privilege . . . if the services of the psychotherapist were sought or obtained to enable or aid anyone to commit or plan to commit a crime or a tort or to escape detection or apprehension after the commission of a crime or a tort."

still provides a shield, even though the interests of the criminal justice system are compelling.

Applying the first exception, the California Supreme Court rejected Oziel's claim of privilege for the tape recordings that covered two of the therapy sessions, one with each of the brothers. Mosk noted that the "dangerous patient" exception has the same purpose as the *Tarasoff* rule, and he reaffirmed *Tarasoff*'s resolution of the conflict between public and private values: "The protective privilege ends where the public peril begins."[13] Oziel did have reasonable cause to believe that Lyle and Erik were dangerous to him, Mosk finds, and also indirectly dangerous to his wife and lover (each of whom had been involved in his professional practice). Oziel also had cause to believe that disclosure to the two women was necessary to prevent any harm, and he did disclose to them all the communications reflected on audiotape. The Supreme Court therefore affirmed the trial court's conclusion that the conditions of the exception were met and the privilege did not apply.

However, the high court found that the conditions of the exception were not met with respect to material from the other two sessions because Oziel lacked reason to believe that disclosure was necessary. It also rejected the idea that the tapes were not privileged under the "crime or tort" exception. The

---

13. 3 Cal. 4th at p. 452. Subsequent citations of the *Menendez* opinion are by parenthetical page references in the text.

Court of Appeal (the intermediate appellate court)
had concluded that Oziel was motivated by self-
preservation when he made the tapes, the Menendez
brothers were motivated by self-interest, and "[t]he
purported 'therapy' was, in fact, a charade" (p. 454).
The Supreme Court rejected this reasoning:

> It appears that in virtually all psychotherapy what
> motivates the participants is *not* psychotherapy for
> its own sake. For example, the psychotherapist is
> sometimes motivated by self-interest, as when he
> earns his living solely through his practice. For his
> part, the patient is sometimes motivated by self-
> preservation, as when he struggles to resist the
> temptation of suicide or antisocial conduct. As a
> general matter, the dispositional fact is *what* the
> participants do, not *why*. [p. 454]

Without revealing their contents, Mosk went on
to affirm the trial court's conclusion that the sessions had indeed been "for the purpose of therapy"
(p. 454).

As in *Lifschutz*, the court here staves off attempts
to diminish the psychotherapist-patient privilege by
expanding the reach of the exceptions. It affirms
that "the purpose [of the privilege] is indeed to grant
[the patient] power to bar evidence—in order to
protect his right to privacy and promote the psychotherapeutic relationship" (p. 448). It gives teeth to
this pronouncement by excluding two of the tapes,
including the only one with actual statements by
the two defendants.

The absence of any clear account of exactly *how* confidentiality "promotes the psychotherapeutic relationship" remains a weakness in both cases, however. As Mosk's peculiar discussion of the "crime or tort" exception suggests, the court still has only a vague idea of what takes place in the therapist's office. This conceptual weakness may not be harmful where the patient voluntarily waives his privacy, as Housek did, and where the threatened intrusion is scrupulously limited, as it is in both *Lifschutz* and *Menendez*.

However, the opinions do not let us forget that the court is in the business not just of protecting patients but of weighing conflicting values. "We do not face the alternatives of enshrouding the patient's communication to the psychotherapist in the black veil of absolute privilege or of exposing it to the white glare of absolute publicity. Our choice lies, rather, in the grey area" (*Lifschutz*, p. 422). In both *Tarasoff* and *Menendez*, the court confronted a "public peril." Where the sense of such peril produces the child abuse reporting laws, the vagueness about psychotherapeutic process allows much more serious erosion of the privilege and therefore also of the patient's privacy. The threat of that erosion is apparent, if not fully realized, in the *Stritzinger* case.[14]

---

14. *People* v. *Stritzinger* (1983) 34 Cal 3d 505. Subsequent references to the opinion are by parenthetical page numbers in the text.

The defendant in this case was charged with molesting his 14-year-old stepdaughter, Sarah. Both Stritzinger himself and Sarah had consulted a clinical psychologist, Dr. Walker, and in a session with Walker, Sarah revealed that she had engaged in sexual activity with her stepfather. Complying with the reporting law, Walker reported the conversation to the child welfare agency, which in turn relayed the information to the sheriff.

A deputy then spoke on the telephone to Walker, who repeated the substance of his discussion with Sarah and also informed the deputy that he was to meet with Stritzinger himself later that day. That session took place, and in it, Stritzinger confirmed what Sarah had already told Walker about their sexual relations. After the session, the deputy again called Walker, who was reluctant to disclose what Stritzinger had said. After the deputy read him a section of the reporting statute, however, Walker did recount the substance of Stritzinger's session. This telephone conversation was recorded, and a written summary was also prepared.

At trial, Walker testified, over objection, about Stritzinger's therapy session with him, and the written report summarizing his conversation with the deputy was used to refresh his memory. Stritzinger was convicted of various counts of felony and misdemeanor child molestation. However, the California Supreme Court reversed his conviction on the grounds that the therapist's testimony should not have been admitted. The court found that Walker complied fully with his legal obligation when he reported the information he learned from Sarah. Since he learned of no additional instances of molestation from Stritzinger, the contents of his session with Stritzinger were protected by the psychotherapist–patient privilege.

In a separate, concurring opinion, Justice Kaus stated that he would have gone further, and his opinion underlines the danger averted in this case on extremely narrow grounds: only because Stritzinger revealed no additional sexual activity in his session with Walker. Kaus argued that any statements in therapy should remain privileged unless the patient had been warned at the outset that the doctor intended to reveal the contents of the session. "[T]here is obviously something revolting," he wrote, "about the spectacle of a psychotherapist testifying to a patient's confidences in a criminal action in which the patient is the defendant" (pp. 521–522).

Unlike the majority, which took refuge in the peculiar facts of the case, Kaus recognized that the reporting law not only threatened to nullify the psychotherapist–patient privilege but had grave implications for the practice of psychotherapy:

> In the area of sexual abuse of children by adults, the law, presumably, has three objectives: to punish the abuser, to identify and protect his victims, and to cure him in order to protect future potential victims. Since it is fair to assume that child

molesters like to avoid being prosecuted just as much as other criminals, it obviously impedes the objective of cure if therapists who are supposed to effect it are legally bound to testify against their patients in court. Those who do so a few times should not plan on specializing in pedophilia. [p. 523]

It is to the origins of the reporting laws that we now turn.

2

ABSENT AT
THE CREATION

2

ABSENT AT
THE CREATION

In October 1986, Michael Searcy took his daughter Stacy home with him to California from Texas. Stacy had been living there with her mother Sandra, from whom Searcy was divorced.[1] In California, Searcy hired Roy R. Auerbach, a licensed clinical psychologist, to examine Stacy. Auerbach subsequently gave Searcy a written opinion stating his

---

1. See *Searcy* v. *Auerbach* (9th Cir. 1992), 980 F.2d 609. Subsequent references are in parentheses in the text. It is not clear from the published opinion whether Michael Searcy took Stacy to California without his ex-wife's consent or knowledge or why he provided Auerbach's statement to the Texas authorities.

belief that Stacy had been sexually abused while in her mother's custody.

Searcy contacted the police and a child welfare agency in Houston in early 1987 and gave them Auerbach's opinion. The Texas officials called their counterparts in California. According to Sandra Searcy's lawyers, they also investigated the allegations and found them groundless (Goldberg 1992). The California officials called Auerbach, who repeated to them the statements he had made in his opinion. After Sandra Searcy obtained a copy of the opinions, she and her children sued Auerbach in United States District Court for libel, professional negligence, and intentional infliction of emotional distress.

Auerbach argued that the California Child Abuse and Neglect Reporting Act immunized him from such a suit, and the district court agreed. However, the Searcys appealed, and the Ninth Circuit Court of Appeals reversed the district court's ruling. Auerbach's lawyers argued that the report to Searcy was authorized and therefore protected because it would be an intermediate step toward notifying the proper authorities, but Judge John T. Noonan rejected this flexible approach to the reporting law. He pointed out that the law required Auerbach to report suspected abuse not to a layperson such as Michael Searcy but to a child protective agency, and concluded that only the reports specifically required by the statute were protected. Since Auerbach had failed to notify the police or the county welfare department, "[i]mmunity he lacks" (p. 611). Accordingly, the Ninth Circuit returned the case to the district court for trial.

Auerbach's predicament illustrates some of the dangers that the reporting laws bring to the practice of psychology. These dangers go beyond the ethical conflict that arises when a psychotherapist must report a patient's confidential statements to policemen and public agencies. Sandra Searcy's tort claims would now go to trial, and Auerbach may be liable for civil damages. In addition, as Judge Noonan indicated, Auerbach violated the reporting statute twice: once by failing to notify the authorities and once by providing the report to Michael Searcy, who was not authorized to receive it. The psychologist is therefore subject to criminal as well as civil penalties.

The reporting laws do not apply to psychologists alone; psychiatrists, social workers, marriage and family counselors, and a host of others[2] are all

---

2. Penal Code section 11165.7 lists the "child care custodians" required to report, including the following: teacher, instructional aide, teacher's aide or assistant, day-care worker, Head Start teacher, administrator of a public or private day camp, social worker, probation officer. Section 11165.8 adds "health practitioners": physician and surgeon, psychiatrist, psychologist, dentist, resident, intern, podiatrist, chiropractor, licensed nurse, dental hygienist, optometrist, marriage, family and child counselor, paramedic, psychological assistant, family and child counselor trainee, state or county public health employee, coroner, medical examiner,

equally vulnerable, as are the agencies that employ them. Indeed, a Massachusetts jury recently awarded $100,000 (the maximum possible from a public agency) to a man falsely accused of molesting his daughter by a caseworker from the State Department of Social Services (Grunwald 1995). Surely a law that jeopardizes so sharply a large group of respected professionals would have been controversial from the start—with those directly threatened, if not with the general public.

In fact, nothing could be further from the truth. Starting in the early 1960s, child abuse reporting laws were passed with remarkable speed and with no opposition worth mentioning in states across the nation, including California. As one study of the reporting laws puts it, "Seldom in the nation's history has a specific kind of legislation been enacted so quickly in so many states" (Paulsen et al. 1966, p. 482). How does one explain this extraordinary growth? One writer finds the key in expanded connections between law, social work, and psychology, especially psychology with a "family system" perspective (Weisberg 1984).[3] This account empha-

---

and religious practitioner who diagnoses, examines, or treats children.

3. Weisberg describes three different phases of expert influence on policy regarding adult sexual misconduct toward children: (1) the 1930s, when the first recognition of psychiatry as a science led to widespread use of the term *sexual psychopath* to define offenders; (2) the 1950s, when criminal terminology became more prominent and psychiatrists

sizes the influence of such figures as Henry Giaretto, a California marriage and family counselor who developed a child sexual abuse treatment program in Santa Clara County. Giaretto's program was energetically publicized, supported (after 1975) with state funds, and eventually imitated in several other states (Weisberg 1984).

Treatment programs do not receive state money without public awareness that a problem exists, of course. Television did much to create that awareness. For example, in a "dramatic and heart-rending" (Paulsen et al. 1966, p. 488) episode of the "Ben Casey" television series in 1963, two young children die because no one reports the behavior of their dangerously disturbed mother to the authorities. Such programs had a large audience, and legislators were mindful of their influence. For example, on May 13, 1963, Assemblyman Cologne of Riverside County wrote to Governor Edmund G. Brown urging him to support AB 534, an early version of the reporting law. The assemblyman noted, "This matter . . . was featured in a recent television show on the Ben Casey series. There is a great deal of public sympathy in favor of its purpose."

The press and popular fiction have also done their part to arouse the public. "Child abuse—it's getting worse," warned the *San Francisco Sunday*

---

began to admit that diagnosis and treatment were difficult; and (3) the 1970s, when psychologists committed to family counseling and social workers became more influential.

Examiner & Chronicle in an April 24, 1977 edito-
rial (cf. Paulsen et al. 1966). Fifteen years later and
just as urgently, the front page of another paper reported "outrage over the light sentences being given
to child molesters." The story goes on to cite the belief of unnamed "criminal justice experts" that
"[j]udges, prosecutors, and law enforcement officers need to take child molestation cases and sex
crimes more seriously." (See "Crimes clog the
courts," *Oakland Tribune*, Dec. 13, 1992, p. 1.) Such
crimes figure prominently in novels like Pat
Conroy's best-selling *The Prince of Tides* (also a successful film), where the hero is cured of his depression after he tells a psychotherapist about having
been raped as a child.

Mental health professionals have responded to
this climate with conferences, journals, and a growing mountain of scholarly material on child abuse
and "victimology." Ten years ago, a bibliography
listed 58 of these studies (Mrazek 1983). A book
published five years later cites nearly 500 and does
not include such influential but less scholarly works
as Alice Miller's (Haugaard and Reppucci 1988). In
a society where "the problems of child abuse are
becoming more prevalent and acknowledged,"[4]

---

4. California Senate Resolution No. 24, introduced February 21, 1986, calling for the establishment of a Task Force
on Child Abuse and the Schools. Among other matters, the
task force was to consider "the need for a uniform statewide
reporting system."

where a father's photographs of his nude 6-year-old daughter (taken to complete a photography class assignment) can produce a child pornography prosecution and conviction (Carvajal 1995), no politician wants to stand anywhere but with the helpless and innocent victims. Reporting laws are an obvious way for the legislature to show that it takes "child molestation cases and sex crimes" very seriously indeed.

To map out the powerful, intertwined beliefs about sexuality, children, and punishment that give life to this continuing national preoccupation is beyond the scope of our study. Its primary concern is with the effect of the reporting laws, not their cultural and social origins (although we have some thoughts about the latter in Chapter 4). However, it is useful to identify some of the political forces that shaped those laws in California, where "child sexual abuse" was first recognized in a statute.[5] In California, as we shall see, except for one or two formulaic expressions of assent by professional groups, psychologists and psychiatrists played no advisory role whatsoever.

Their nearly total absence from the legislative process represents a missed opportunity to preserve the confidentiality so important to the practice of

---

5. According to Weisberg (1984) the term *child sexual abuse* was first enacted into law in the 1975 California statute that provided funding for the Santa Clara program and encouraged the establishment of similar centers in other counties.

their profession. At the same time, the history of that process reveals the kind of work that must be done if the patient's right to confidentiality is to be restored. Such work might also prevent damage to other important relationships. In testimony more than ten years ago before a committee of the California Assembly, Deputy Attorney General Michael Gates expressed the belief that more informants were needed. "We have expanded the number of people to report. Every year there is always somebody else that you want to put in there that you have overlooked."[6]

California's first reporting law did not relieve public anxiety about child abuse or put an end to the belief that much abuse went unreported. In the 1978 Maddy hearings on proposed amendments of the law, hearings dominated by law enforcement bureaucrats,[7] one finds claim after claim of "some very serious problems of underreporting" (p. 25):

---

6. Transcript of hearing on SB 1614, Assembly Committee on Criminal Justice, Kenneth L. Maddy, Chairman, November 21, 1978, p. 26. Subsequent references to this transcript are in parentheses in the text.
7. The witness list includes a deputy attorney general, the director of the state Crime Prevention Unit, and representatives from the Department of Justice, the Juvenile Officers' Association, and the Juvenile Section of the Los Angeles County Counsel's office. There were also witnesses from the state Department of Social Services and from hospital and physician groups.

We have been advised that . . . down in San Bernardino . . . reports of child molestation—any type of sexual assault on the child—are not being reported. In other words a child comes in and tells a marriage and family counselor that "I'm having an incestuous relationship with my father." Maybe not exactly in those terms. Because of philosophical hangup, in terms of involving the bureaucracies or the local agencies who are responsible, it's not being reported. [p. 25]

Whatever its deficiencies, such evidence has shaped the law, leading to stiffer reporting requirements, penalties, and an increasingly long list of those required to report. These changes have had a predictable effect. In 1974, a total of 53,919 abuse cases were referred to county child protective services in California.[8] In 1984, the figure was 250,813; in 1991, it was 571,241.[9] It is worth noting that these figures cover *all* abuse, including the largest two categories, physical abuse and general neglect.

---

8. California Center for Health Statistics, Report on Specialized Child Protective Services for California, 1974.

9. See "Child Abuse Incidents in California," a chart prepared by the Statistical Services Branch of the State Department of Social Services and included in a pamphlet on the reporting law prepared by that department for "health practitioners." The 1991 figure is taken from the Order Granting Injunctive Relief (February 9, 1993) in *People of the State of California ex rel. Anderson* v. *Sullivan*, No.C-92-3930-VRW (N.D. Cal.).

Sexual abuse was involved in less than 20 percent of the reported cases.

A large bureaucracy is needed to handle such an avalanche of reports. Bureaucracies cost money, and it is not surprising that money is a recurrent theme in legislative hearings on the reporting law. Although individual states took the initiative in passing these laws, the federal government provided a powerful financial spur in the 1974 Child Abuse Prevention and Treatment Act. Under the act and a related grant program, a state may qualify for federal child abuse grants only if it "provide[s] for the reporting of known *or suspected* instances of child abuse and neglect" (emphasis added).[10]

The wish to obtain these funds rings like a refrain through the history of the California laws. California first applied for the funds in 1974. It received approval for a grant of $269,000 to fund "special pilot projects" in 1977,[11] but officials wor-

---

10. See 45 Code of Federal Regulations section 1340.3(2)(i). The section also provides: "This requirement shall be deemed satisfied if a state requires specified persons by law, and has a law or administrative procedure which requires, allows, or encourages *all other citizens*, to report known or suspected incidences of child abuse and neglect to one or more properly constituted authorities with the power and responsibility to perform an investigation and take necessary ameliorative and protective steps" (emphasis added).

11. This history is taken from the "Policy Paper Regarding Child Abuse Hearings" in the legislative bill file of the Senate Judiciary Committee. The file includes material on As-

ried about the state's continuing eligibility. In the same year, in response to a request from the director of the state Department of Health, the California attorney general issued an opinion. Even though the California statute then in existence did not refer explicitly to "suspected" abuse, the attorney general concluded that the requirement to report such abuse was implied.[12]

This reassurance was not enough, however. In 1978, testifying before the Maddy committee, Deputy Attorney General Gates tried to explain why the existing law was too vague about the circumstances that require a report: "Only with suspicion. You don't have to be judge and jury [or] talk about probable cause [in order] to make a report. We want them to report things they suspect, not that they can go out and get a search warrant or an arrest warrant [sic]" (p. 18). The statute was duly amended in 1980 to close the potential loophole[13] and, of

---

sembly Bill 1058 (1977), containing various amendments to the reporting law.

12. See Opinion Letter CV 76/259 IL, issued February 8, 1977, citing a study in the *Journal of the State Bar*, which concluded that the California law was based on a model statute drafted and promulgated by the Children's Bureau of the U.S. Department of Health, Education, and Welfare.

13. The amended statute imposes a duty to report when a health practitioner "has knowledge of or observes" a child and "knows or reasonably suspects" that abuse has occurred (California Penal Code section 11166).

course, to guarantee that California could continue to receive the federal funds.[14]

Financial pressure cannot be separated from bureaucratic pressure. The legislative record reveals recurrent turf wars between different professional groups and agencies, all competing for the legislative dollar and the authority and prestige that go with it. In California, one of the casualties of these wars was the discretion originally granted to physicians when they encountered evidence of abuse.

The original 1963 reporting law "allow[ed] the doctor to determine whether to report, [so] it seem[ed] unlikely that a court could convict him for not reporting."[15] A recurrent theme in the 1978

---

14. Another episode in this tale unfolded recently. The U.S. Department of Health and Human Services (HHS) informed California that it would recommend denial of a $1.8 million child abuse grant because the state allegedly failed to meet federal requirements. California obtained relief in federal court. Noting the volume of reports in California and concluding that without the funds, "the state and its children will suffer irreparable harm," the court issued an injunction preventing HHS from withholding the funds or distributing them to other states [Order Granting Injunctive Relief, February 9, 1993, *People of the State of California ex rel. Anderson* v. *Sullivan*, No. C-92-3930-VRW (N.D. Cal)].

15. *Journal of the State Bar*, review of 1963 legislation, p. 763. However, in the case of *Landeros* v. *Flood*, 17 Cal.3d 399 (1976), the California Supreme Court established civil liability for a doctor's failure to report.

hearings is distrust of such individual judgment and resentment of the discretion given to doctors.

> We want to close those loopholes and involve everybody in the process. Whereby if in fact the decision to intervene or not intervene or to proceed formally or informally is going to be made, it is made by all parties that are responsible and not just one person. Whether it's a peace officer or a social worker or a doctor or anybody else. Nobody has the right to make that kind of judgment. [p. 26]

> We in the Attorney General's Office strongly oppose any effort to allow single specialized groups to presume to make all the judgments necessary to protect the safety of children in child abuse cases. [p. 31]

> All of these [decisions] have to be made by a collective judgment, and by having a complete, accurate index, a central index, then this assists those people who make judgments in terms of how they are going to proceed with that judgment" [p. 44].

These witnesses put their faith in "team-building" and "interagency cooperation" (p. 27), and there is a strong bias against the "single specialized groups"— there is no need to identify them by name—who "argue that child abuse is not a crime but a noncriminal problem best handled by treatment" (p. 31). If any one kind of expertise deserves special recognition and authority, it is not that of doctors (no one mentions psychotherapists) but of the police. "There are many practical and compelling factors which uniquely qualify law enforcement for its role in child abuse handling" (p. 33).

Doctors could see that their primacy was threatened. One pediatrician wrote to an assemblyman who proposed that reports should be made to an interdisciplinary team, not just a police department: "I gather that the police have been leaders in opposition and it is wryly amusing to me as a physician to see that it is not only doctors who like to run away with the whole show."[16] In the end, the police have indeed run away, if not with the whole show, then with a large part of it. Under the current California statute, reports must be made either to a police or sheriff's department or a county welfare department.[17] After the report is made, other interested agencies in each county are to "implement cooperative arrangements" for investigating the suspected child abuse.[18]

---

16. Letter dated June 24, 1977 from Talcott Bates, M.D. to Assemblyman Bill Lockyer regarding proposed bill AB 1058. Dr. Bates was correct. One law enforcement group wrote to Assemblyman Lockyer that it opposed his bill for the following reason: "The membership of the Child Abuse Reporting Team is biased toward non-investigative personnel. Health professionals are treatment oriented and do not really belong in an investigative function." Letter dated May 17, 1977 from Esther A. Cardall, Chair, San Diego County Inter-Agency Youth Advisory Committee.

17. Penal Code sections 11166 and 11165.9.

18. Penal Code section 11166.3.

Public outcry, professional competition, and the hunger for federal dollars all favor "putting more teeth"[19] into the reporting law. However, certain professional groups, alert to the danger of interference with their work, have been able to remove a molar or two. California teachers expressed their concern that responses to disruptive students could be construed as child abuse and reported to the authorities. In response, the legislature amended the statute so that the term *child protective agency* does not include school district police or security workers and the term *child abuse* does not apply to efforts by such authorities to control unruly students.[20]

Physicians, similarly, were concerned that one section of the statute would force them to report any evidence (such as a request for birth control pills) that a female patient under the age of 18 had engaged in sexual relations, even if consensual.[21]

---

19. The phrase is taken from the Third Reading analysis of proposed SB 1614 (a version of the reporting law that did not pass into law) prepared by the Senate Republican Caucus, dated May 12, 1978, p. 3.

20. Cal. Penal Code sections 11165.9 and 11165.4. See also Analysis of SB 646 prepared for the California Senate Committee on Judiciary, Hearing Date, May 12, 1987.

21. See "Background on California's new Child Abuse Reporting Law" (unpublished) prepared by Simon Haines, Associate Director, California Medical Association, Division of Government Relations, February 2, 1981. Haines discusses a case (that never came to trial) in which a pediatrician was charged with failure to report child abuse after he referred a pregnant minor to an obstetrician without notifying the authorities.

Although one amendment to delete the provision
in question failed under intense lobbying by anti-
abortion groups, including the Committee on Moral
Concerns,[22] it was quietly dropped in subsequent
legislative action.

In light of these successful efforts to limit the
scope of the California law, it is surprising that
psychotherapists, more seriously affected by that
law than teachers or physicians, had so little to say
about its enactment. Psychologists and psychiatrists did not appear before committees of the legislature to testify about the law or to articulate their
professional concerns. In particular, there is no
testimony, from them or from anyone else, about
erosion of confidentiality or the possible effects of
that erosion on the practice of psychotherapy. In
the absence of such lobbying, California has a reporting law that turns the principle of confidentiality
on its head. Instead of protection for the patient
who discloses his private life to a psychotherapist,
there is protection for the psychotherapist (or for
anyone else) who makes a report under the law—
protection, that is, for the informant.[23]

The only expression of concern in the legislative
record for the tradition of confidentiality comes

22. See Haines, "Background," pp. 7–8.
23. "The identity of all persons who report . . . shall be confidential and disclosed only between child protective agencies, or to counsel representing a child protective agency"
[Penal Code section 11167(d)].

from a college student writing a term paper on child abuse. Noting the proposal to add psychologists and marriage counselors to the list of required reporters, she wrote, "I am wondering if this would hamper the confidentiality that presently exists between client and psychotherapist."[24] Apparently, this question failed to trouble the California Psychological Association. The legislative chairman of that group also wrote about the proposal, but only to make sure that psychologists were included in the final bill.[25]

The California reporting laws have spawned a small industry of programs to educate psychotherapists about their legal responsibilities. There is a captive market for such programs. The hypothetical cases that confront candidates on the oral section of the psychology licensing examination routinely include a reporting situation. In addition, candidates are required by the state to spend a Saturday at, for example, the University of Califor-

---

24. Letter dated October 22, 1977 from Joann Matheus to Assemblyman Lockyer regarded proposed AB 1058. There is no copy of a reply in the legislative files.
25. The letter reads in its entirety as follows: "I have reviewed the May 23 amended version of AB 1058 and have noticed that psychologists have been eliminated from the list of those who must report. In the original bill, psychologist appeared on line 22 of page 2. I would appreciate psychologist being included in an amended bill." Letter dated June 3, 1977 from Dr. Lewis Carpenter, Jr. to Assemblyman Lockyer regarding proposed AB 1058.

nia Extension Division. There, for a fee, they will learn how to recognize and treat the symptoms of child abuse and, not incidentally, how to comply with the reporting law.

Some of these courses brush aside the ethical conflict created by the reporting laws, not to mention any clinical consequences. When a child is afraid that talking about an incident will send her father to jail, some candidates are taught, the psychotherapist need only explain that the father needs help, and a report to the authorities will guarantee that he gets it. Such was the answer to one student in a course we attended, where written handouts took the same approach.[26] The instructor had no suggestion about how to maintain the child's confidence in the psychotherapist in the event that legal proceedings against the offending relative actually began. Discussion was confined to the question of how to comply with the reporting requirement and how to make sure that the patient made the necessary disclosure.

This posture of diligent compliance finds scholarly defenders in the professional mainstream. One substantial study published by the American Psy-

---

26. The written material included a guide prepared by the Sexual Assault Center at Harborview Medical Center, Seattle. "Be aware that the child . . . will be very reluctant and full of anxiety. . . . The fears often need to be allayed. 'It's not bad to tell what happened.' 'You won't get into trouble.' 'You can help your dad by telling what happened.'"

chological Association itself amounts to an extended apologia for the reporting laws. Failing to
see any conflict between the policeman's role and
the therapist's, the author argues that compliance
is in the best interests of patients and therefore
presents no ethical dilemma at all (Kalichman
1993).

Other scholars are more sensitive to both ethical and clinical dilemmas. For example, several
studies recognize that the issue of informed consent is especially complex when children are involved. Renshaw (1987) asks whether it is possible
for a child to give informed consent to answer questions about sexual history. Haugaard and Reppucci
(1988) suggest that it is unethical for a clinician not
to inform a child that reporting as required by law
"will subsequently result in an intrusion of some
sort . . . into the child's family life" and that failure
to inform "may result in damaging the clinician/
child relationship" (pp. 143–144). Since telling a
child about the reporting laws "may stifle some of
the child's descriptions" (p. 169) there is a direct
conflict between a psychotherapist's ethical obligations and the needs of the police. In Haugaard and
Reppucci's study, awareness of these obligations
coexists uneasily with a belief that the clinician
should remain "a source of viable information in
the legal process" (p. 180). At times, Haugaard and
Reppucci seem unaware of conflicts between clinical and legal values. For example, they acknowledge
that a clinician must be careful not to discourage

the loving feelings that an incestuously abused girl may experience toward her father "after an initial period of anger and hatred," so that the patient does not "come to believe that only certain emotions are acceptable" (pp. 190–191). They do not point out that such avoidance of "punitive emotional reactions" is in direct conflict with the clinician's obligation to report the incest.

Some psychotherapists simply refuse to report. Haugaard and Reppucci cite two unpublished studies. One indicated that 25 percent of a sample of nonlicensed mental health professionals would not report a confirmed case of incestuous abuse (Kalichman and Craig 1987). The other study found that clinicians in New York City were reluctant to report suspected child sexual abuse because they believed such reports did more harm than good (Alfaro 1985). Others insist that a clinician cannot faithfully serve both a patient and the legal system and should not accept such a dual role (Goldstein et al. 1986). A study at the Johns Hopkins Sexual Disorders Clinic suggests that, at least for some patients, the perception of a psychotherapist's divided loyalties makes treatment impossible. The study covered periods before and after 1989, when the state of Maryland implemented a new law that required reporting of all disclosures by adult patients about child sexual abuse. (The previous law required a report only if a physician suspected abuse when examining a child.) The authors of this study conclude that the new law produced none of the intended benefits. First, it deterred undetected adult abusers from entering treatment, and "[o]ne cannot intervene clinically if individuals who need help refrain from identifying themselves in the first place." In addition, the reporting law deterred patients from disclosing sexual abuse that occurred during treatment, and, perhaps most important, failed to increase the number of abused children who could be identified. "Mandatory reporting, at least insofar as its effects on a large sexual disorders clinic are concerned, has not led to identification of even a single child at risk" (Berlin et al. 1991, p. 452).

The Johns Hopkins study notes that "[m]andatory reporting, by superseding privilege, significantly alters the psychiatrist–patient relationship" (p. 452). However, the authors do not explain how or why that relationship is altered, and, indeed, the literature offers little in the way of such accounts. Haugaard and Reppucci (1988) cite an unpublished study of a sexual abuse case in Jordan, Minnesota. "'One psychotherapist said that the biggest mistake she made was telling the children that "everything would be fine" if they told the truth; when she then turned to the police with information the children had given her and the cases got dismissed, . . . the children became resentful and bitter, and the treatment process was set back dramatically'" (Tester 1986, p. 15).

Such an anecdote is suggestive but lacks much emotional depth. There is a story by Chekhov, "A

Trifling Occurrence," that gives a richer sense of
what children may feel when their confidence is
betrayed. In this story, a wealthy young landowner
named Bieliayev visits the house of his mistress, a
woman with two children who is separated from
her husband. She is not home, so Bieliayev waits
in the drawing room and talks to her young son
Aliosha. Bieliayev "had never once turned his attention to the boy and had completely ignored his existence." On this occasion, however, he initiates a
friendly chat. Aliosha carelessly says something
that suggests he is in contact with his father, and
Bieliayev pursues the hint.

> "But, be honest—on your honour. By your face I
> can see you're not telling me the truth. If you made
> a slip of the tongue by mistake, what's the use of
> shuffling. Tell me, do you see him? As one friend
> to another."
> Aliosha mused.
> "And you won't tell Mother?" he asked.
> "What next."
> "On your word of honour."
> "My word of honour."
> "Swear an oath."

Thus reassured, Aliosha tells the whole story: the
children's nurse takes them often to a sweetshop
where their father meets them and buys them
treats. The father, it seems, is unhappy about the
separation and tells the children that Bieliayev has
"ruined" their mother.

Bieliayev is indignant, and when Aliosha's mother comes in with her other child, in spite of the boy's frantic gestures, he promptly tells her everything. The mother runs out to confront the nurse, leaving Bieliayev alone with the children.

> He was absorbed in his insult, and now, as before, he did not notice the presence of the boy. He, a big serious man, had nothing to do with boys. And Aliosha sat down in a corner and in terror told Sonya how he had been deceived. He trembled, stammered, wept.

Chekhov is not writing about psychotherapy, of course, and his tale of a confidence casually obtained and just as casually betrayed is some distance from the issues addressed by the reporting laws. However, the situation in his story is analogous. Bieliayev puts his grotesque sense of injury before his promise to keep Aliosha's secret: "'This is something more important than any words of honour.'" In the same way, proponents of the reporting laws place the legal system's hunger for information before the aims of psychotherapy and the confidentiality that makes it possible to achieve them.

Moreover, Chekhov's story suggests some of what is missing from discussion of the reporting laws. If psychotherapists are to challenge those laws, they must provide a detailed and theoretically coherent account of what the laws actually do to

the relationship between patient and psychotherapist—and not just, as in the Hopkins study, where
that relationship takes place in a sexual disorders
clinic. To put the question more precisely, what
happens to the transference and to other features
of the treatment when a psychotherapist tells the
patient that certain kinds of disclosures will be reported to the authorities? Our next chapter addresses this question.

3

LOSS OF
CONFIDENCE

Psychoanalysis cannot function if the patient does not have complete confidence that what he says to his psychoanalyst is privileged. Because the term *psychoanalysis* is used by all kinds of "therapists" it cannot be assumed that what we mean by the psychoanalytic method is self-evident. It differs in striking ways from other forms of talking treatments.

Psychoanalysts and psychoanalytic psychotherapists[1] encourage patients to free-associate: to say as openly and uncritically as possible whatever crosses their mind. Much as many new patients

---

1. *Psychoanalysis* refers, from this point on in our text, to psychoanalysis and to psychoanalytic psychotherapy.

might wish to organize a session according to a pre-
determined agenda—and it is quite common for
beginners to decide beforehand what they want to
talk about—the analyst does not ordinarily collude
with this aim. He may suggest that an agenda seems
a way to escape the uncertainties of talking freely.
Or he may remain quiet, allowing the patient to
discover that an agenda does not work for very long;
the absence of the analyst's conversational response, the passing of time in the hour, the arrival
of other—unplanned—thoughts naturally break
down the structure of premeditation.

The people, places, and events that occur to the
analysand do not have the same status that is assumed in ordinary conversation. A patient may be
complaining about a friend who always keeps his
distance; the analyst may take this friend to be an
objective metaphor of an aspect of the patient that
is functioning at that very moment in relation to
the analyst. "I think you are perplexed by your remove from me," the analyst may reply. Or he may
consider the patient's removed friend to be the
patient's unconscious perception of the analyst,
leading him to say, "I think you are also irked by
your experience of my silence." Usually he remains
quiet, allowing the march of free associations to
establish their mysterious logic, waiting until what
Freud termed a "tissue of thought" becomes apparent.

The right to say what is on one's mind in psychotherapy is not restricted—as it is in legal or

medical consultations—to the expression of conscious ideas. At the heart of the free-associative process is a method for the unpremeditated disclosure of whatever crosses the patient's mind. In order to do this, he must trust that the clinician will not take him at his word, but will instead regard the expression of thought as the means to liberate unconscious ideas, memories, and feelings that contribute to his mental suffering and disturbed relations. Patients resist the disseminative power of this kind of freedom, often sensing they are on the breach of disclosing something they would prefer to keep private. Nonetheless they know that in order to be analyzed they really must try to push on and say what comes to mind, especially when reluctant to do so.

Were there to be a restriction of this basic process, that is, if the patient felt that he could safely talk about his neediness but could not discuss sexuality or aggression, then the entire procedure would come to a halt. It is not possible to be unconsciously selective in this way. If a patient is heterosexual and overly well behaved but has always been troubled by curiously dissociated pederastic fantasies, the reporting of such fantasies is crucial to an understanding of his unconscious mental life. But if he is afraid that in reporting such fantasies he is bordering on criminal liability, he will keep such thoughts to himself. His self-censorship not only means that a specific area of conflict is not addressed, it also means that he is from this point

incapable of free-associating. When free association is no longer possible because of some external
intrusion into the consulting room that compro-
mises confidentiality, then psychoanalysis exists in
name only; what takes place in the consulting room
is something else.

The psychoanalytic method facilitates the difficult but inevitable arrival of "psychic truth." Free
association does not simply establish what the patient did the previous day, who he talked to, what
tasks he performed, what bright ideas occurred to
him; in the analytic relationship, such seeming facts
of life metamorphose into metaphors of the unconscious. They are its derivatives, and the psychoanalyst comes to understand what he takes to be unconscious thinking by concentrating on the logic of
sequence and the metaphorical potential of each
and every narrative object. So if a patient talks
about his wish to go on a vacation, then discusses
his uncle who broke his leg skiing the previous
week, then talks about his inability to finish tasks
at his work, and concludes by describing what a
meaningless life he seems to have, the analyst will
note a sequence of ideas: wish for vacation, injury
to the body, guilt over failed tasks, and despair. By
this time in his work with the patient, he may know
enough to indicate that the analysand seems to have
abandoned his wish for pleasure because those who
have not done their work should have their legs
broken, an unfortunate thought that leaves him

wondering if he will ever permit himself to take pleasure in life.

With the same sequence of ideas, however, we could construct numerous other equally plausible unconscious ideas, and indeed psychoanalysts frequently debate with one another about which of many interpretations seems to be the correct one at the time. All analysts would agree, however, that the analyst would not interrupt the patient to ask if the uncle was able to walk, or suggest ways in which the patient could complete his work, thereby enabling him (theoretically) to go on vacation.

Some counselors and therapists would directly intervene to comment on the vacation, the uncle, and work as matters of fact that needed to be addressed as such. For a psychoanalyst, however, comments of that kind on such seeming facts of life would destroy their psychic value, that is, their capacity to carry the contents of unconscious thought. Many a counselor and therapist fault psychoanalysts for this reluctance to take facts as things in themselves, but this is not the place for a discussion of the many differences between the therapist and the psychoanalyst. The analyst is not in his mind at least failing to take the patient's life seriously. Indeed, it is his view that only by restraining the kind of response available to the patient from everyone else in life—it is after all easy enough for anyone to get advice from a friend or a different kind of professional—that he can be true to the patient's psychic reality. When this restraint works, the analysand discovers in time that those seeming irritants of the previous day, or the passions of an hour before a session, are important, not as end points of an insight but as evocative mental objects that seem to launch the patient on a totally unexpected and surprisingly revealing journey. What he finds as he travels this distance is not advice on how to live his life, but a vast and complex statement from his internal world, one that establishes his personality in a considered and reflective relation with the other, who now and then brings to the patient's attention those parts of himself that are entangled in self-defeating mires.

No doubt the other course available to counselors and therapists—to advise the client and consider how to deal with the people he discusses in reality—is a valuable form of assistance. Some people would not choose to use psychoanalysis even if they could, and it is important that there be a generous choice of alternative forms of assistance. Indeed, as we shall argue in Chapter 5, it is time to make a clearer distinction between those many therapies that are reality interventionist and psychoanalysis. The interventionist therapist would—and does—welcome mandatory reporting requirements and managed care. The active presence of a third—supervisory—party is regarded as an important limit-setting boundary to therapeutic work. This therapist sees himself as a responsive middleman between the needs of the patient and the concerns of society and insurers and is comfortable explaining his place in that reality to his client. He not only has a firm eye on the patient's external reality, he is a part of that reality as he brokers between the patient and the actual persons in the patient's world.

Let us see by further example why the psychoanalyst does not work in this way.

A patient is telling the analyst about a friend who works in a factory and who has been sexually harassed by a co-worker. A therapist might at this point ask if the friend has reported this to the authorities, and the session might take the course of providing details of how the friend can deal with the issue. The therapist may choose to make something of an interpretation by suggesting that the client has shown courage bringing this detail to the therapists attention; the act has resulted in personal empowerment that will now prove to be effective in reality. They might follow the development of the client's friend as she processes the therapist's suggestions, and the entire session would be aimed at the outer world and its goings on.

The psychoanalyst would not intervene. Why remain silent in the face of what may well be a crime? The answer has several parts. First, in what is termed *object relations theory*, it is always assumed that whatever a patient talks about *might* express an unconscious and unwelcome part of the self. So the harassing figure at the friend's place of work might be the first unconscious sign of the patient's verbalization of a part of himself that is sexually attracted to the friend. By selecting the harasser as an object through which to signify this desire, the patient actually unconsciously invites the analyst to condemn this desire by indicating shock or outrage, and by suggesting punitive forms of action. Such indications would have the effect of sealing off the patient's sexuality under a plastic coating of moral authority, bonding the patient and the clinician, but, unfortunately, bonding them in opposition to the expression of sexuality.

Beyond the goal of avoiding an allegiance with one part of the patient's psyche at the expense of another, analysts remain quiet because above all else they need plenty of time to follow the sequence of free associations presented by the analysand. They have been trained over many years not to react in the customary social manner (again, anyone else to whom the patient disclosed this fact would no doubt react with helpful advice) in order to create the possibility for the analysand's psychic reality to *take priority* over all else. Analysts will often remain quiet for an entire hour, and in time patients not only understand but appreciate this respect for the weightiness of the analysand's free associations. Freedom of expression facilitates a progression in most analytical hours from surface thoughts about the day's events to deeper musings when the patient is silent. Such silences are complex inner experiences that call into being and consciousness fragments of thought and feeling that move more like the structure of musical thought than cognition proper. If the patient does not know what this all comes to, he is not concerned about the lack of narrative cohesion during such silences; indeed, the inner releasings afforded by this freedom speak for themselves, as the analysand finds the analytical process supportive of such inner movement. The patient feels increasingly free to say what comes to mind—or to move into the thick of silence—precisely because the analyst does not take it up on its own terms, but remains unreactive and considerate.

Analytical quiet also permits the analyst to imagine silently all the possible meanings of his patient's comments. For if the patient needs the unintrusive atmosphere of analytical solitude in order to exercise this most radical and far-reaching freedom of speech, so too does the analyst require a nonreactive ambience to allow for his own free-moving inner ideas. Freud termed this "evenly suspended attentiveness," and contemporary analysts refer to it as *reverie*. In effect, the analyst—in order to receive the patient's free-associations—does not go in search of meaning. He does not have his own agenda, as it were, in mind as he listens to his patient. He knows from his training that a very special tool of psychoanalysis is his free-associative process evoked by the patient's comments and attitudes. So listening to the above material the analyst may think at first that it is the patient's expression of homosexual desire, but as time passes and other associations occur, this initial idea may be displaced by a new one. Perhaps the patient is asking that a morally censorious part of

her personality be taken on; or perhaps it is a communication from the transference: the patient feels
sexually molested in the workplace of psychoanalysis. Whatever the psychic truth seems to be will
rarely be instantaneously clear. It will take time—
nonreactive time. And in due course those patients
who come to experience and know what psychoanalysis is will find a deep appreciation of the mentality that creates this sort of time and space.

The analyst will, however, eventually come to
interpretation. And if he says, for example, that the
patient finds it easier to talk about her own sexual
feelings for her friend by attributing them to an
aggressive man who deserves condemnation, he has
not rejected the patient's account of her friend's
work harasser. Instead he has decided, as always,
that whatever psychic truths there are in any narrative must take priority for the analysand if psychoanalysis is to function. We hope it is clear that
this is not equivalent to saying that the account of
the friend's sexual harassment is not true. Indeed,
analysts will customarily acknowledge the integrity
of the patient's actual world by saying something
like, "That sounds upsetting," but then turn this account into psychoanalytical material by saying
something like, "But I wonder if this isn't at the
same time your way of talking about something else
that distresses you," which is a tactful preamble to
discussion of psychic reality.

It is a rare patient, however, who enjoys analytical interpretation of unwanted parts of the person-

ality. That is exactly why, for example, the above-imagined patient "puts" the sexual impulse "into" a creep! For a projection to be effective it must find a good container, and so, for this patient to put unwanted aspects of her sexuality into someone else for secure keeping, she must find a good stand-in. What better proxy than a harasser at work whom her female friend has described at some length? Indeed, precisely because most people do find good containers for their projections, it is even more incumbent on psychoanalytic practitioners to stick as rigorously as possible to the interpretation of projection. So the patient may respond to an initial interpretation with a denial and a repetition of the account of the creep at the factory; indeed, she may augment it with a clear and eloquent account of the sexual politics of the situation. She may find the analyst's emphasis offensive and launch into a prolonged attack on what she assumes to be his political attitudes.

If the psychoanalyst has been correct in his interpretation, however, such resistance will often conceal hidden wishes. By throwing the entire gamut of rationalizations at the analyst, the patient may be saying, "Well, what about this argument about such offending sexual impulses?" or "What about that argument against such creepy sides of the human being? Could there be any response other than condemnation?" The patient unknowingly tests the analyst to see if he can be brought into implicit moral condemnation of the offending

part of the self, but in the psychoanalytical relationship no analyst will do this. It is hoped that in time
the patient will feel increasingly secure about expressing her own sexuality. This sense of security
may lead to a discussion about sexual feelings toward her friend, eventually, perhaps, to discussion
of a sadomasochistic erotic fantasy that is prereq-
uisite to orgasm.

It will be seen, then, that psychoanalysts are
aiming not to organize the patient into some form
of action in the actual world, but to organize the
analysis to move deeper and deeper into the
patient's internal world, from description of a friend
who is harassed, to a part of the self that is attracted
to the friend, to another part of the self that finds
the idea of physical brutality from men exciting, to
the specific fantasy of being penetrated by men and
women in the mouth, the anus, and the vagina si-
multaneously, to increasingly conscious urges to
get the analyst to punish the patient. If allowed to
be—to get on in its own curious and inimitable
way—psychoanalysis gets to where it must if it is
to have a chance of clinical effectiveness. But the
present laws, regulatory intrusions, and managed
care interests, if complied with, would spell the end
of psychoanalysis and leave in its vacant space only
those therapies that take life at face value.

Why is this true?

The spirit of these intrusive requirements demands that the clinician take at face value certain
comments by a patient that unwittingly fall into the

catchment area of the reporting requirements. A borderline adolescent deeply angry with her father for his aloofness believes in good faith that she has an actual memory that he fondled her on several occasions. This must be reported to the police. A schizophrenic young man tells his analyst that he intends to kill his mother because she is in the service of Satan. The clinician must take steps to inform the potential victim of a possible act of harm. In some states this would have to be reported to the police. A haunted schizoid man well into an analysis tells a Swedish clinician that ten years ago he robbed a bank; according to Swedish law certain crimes punishable by two or more years imprisonment must be reported by therapists to the police.[2]

To counselors, therapists, and many others for whom the psychoanalytic relationship has always seemed an arcane act of indulgent folly, the psychoanalytic need to maintain confidence—even in such circumstances—on the grounds of preserving the priority of psychic reality will seem even further madness. But if it is allowed that value is to be gained in providing *one* place of refuge for the mentally disturbed to seek help in absolute confidence, then the psychoanalytic argument that there can be *no* mandated intrusions into the clinical space makes enormous sense. The adolescent girl may indeed have been molested by her father, and

2. For a more complete discussion of reporting laws in Sweden, see Chapter 5.

if this proves to be true, the analyst is not disabled from listening to the patient's discussions of how she intends to solve this in her real world. As always, he will not tell her what to do, but he will examine her anxieties and her identifications as they play themselves out in her inner world. It may be, however, that having sexualized her relation to her father, she will have gratified a wish for something intimate between them and in the wake of this sad attempt at self-consolation, find herself in depressive response to his failure.

The schizophrenic man might indeed firm up plans to kill his mother. Psychoanalysts have at their disposal means to place such patients in care—and confiding in other professionals—that does not result in the patient's being turned over to the police. But most frequently, schizophrenics express aggression in terrifying imagery that does not objectify imminent intentions but does almost exactly the opposite: hyperbolic expressions of aggressions that scare them to death and lead them to live in total hostility to their every impulse and desire. Allowing such a patient to talk about killing his mother without dire reaction is exactly what this kind of schizophrenic needs. And finally, those people who have committed crimes but who have been haunted by them and have come for help for different forms of mental illness need to know that the psychoanalyst will not betray them by handing them over to the police.

There are countless good reasons why others would benefit from access to the private details of a therapist–client relationship, and the state legislatures, regulatory agencies, licensing boards, and insurance companies have established their claims. But what is the ultimate difference between one exception to the otherwise assumed right to confidentiality and a hundred exceptions? There can be none. For once a single good reason is established for the abandonment of such a privilege, other equally compelling reasons will be put forward. This is just what has happened. First it was the abused child who had to be protected by mandatory reporting, then the potential victim of a violent crime, then the innocent lover of a human immunodeficiency virus (HIV) client, and the list is now growing as different groups submit claims for protection. The "duty to protect" has now spread its wings to include an increasing number of people who would benefit from clinical informants.

Young clinicians in training are now learning to cooperate actively with laws, regulations, and health care inquiries in a culture that has lost its sense that confidentiality is indispensable to the practice of psychotherapy. What they are taught reflects the institutional compliance of organizations like the American Psychological Association, which recently declared in a public statement that "the social policy of protecting children from child abuse outweighs the social policies supporting the

protection of confidentiality in the therapy relationship" (Walker et al. 1989, p. 11). This compliance
in turn reflects an erosion within the profession of
the belief that an analyst's primary duty, like a
lawyer's, a physician's, or a priest's, is toward the
individual who seeks professional help, not toward
society or some conception of society's needs or
goals. There is also a slide into self-deception and
doublethink. We find one clinician who justifies his
disclosure of confidences by telling himself and his
colleagues that a patient he sees for consultation
rather than treatment is not really a patient, so that
disclosure is acceptable (personal communication
to author, 1994), and another who concludes more
sweepingly that "a case can be made for the position that mandated reporting [of molestation] is not
an ethical dilemma at all" (Kalichman 1993, p. 59).
Perhaps the case can be made, but such a position
violates principles that have long seemed axiomatic, and not just in psychotherapy.

When a person seeks pastoral counseling, legal
advice, or a medical examination, it is understood
that he or she has the right to a private consultation, one safeguarded against intrusion at all costs.
Knowing that the consultation is strictly private, the
individual is free to disclose anything he needs to
and in turn to gain help from a qualified professional. The right to this process transcends any
claims on the content of the disclosed. A lawyer or
priest will not subsequently state to the person that
the right of privacy ended with the disclosure of

content x; the right covers all content. The right to such privacy is vital to the function of verbal freedom, which is understood across these important disciplines—law, the clergy, and in some cases medicine—as essential to the possible salvation of a soul in its carnal, theological, or secular world. Salvation is not guaranteed. But each person has the right to seek a professional for a privileged discussion that might lead to his or her redemption.

People who have at least some contact with their inner life are troubled by primal fantasies, thoughts that derive from the magical views of the small child who attacks the mother's body, violently attacks the parental couple, and commits atrocities against rivals for affection. Psychoanalysis has always taken the view that the way to help those individuals who have dealt with such universal unconscious fantasies by pathological means—that is, by overly defending against them, or turning them into perverse actions—is to facilitate free-associative thinking, which brings the unconscious ideas into utterance. Talking the unbearable actually helps in its own right and is part of the therapeutic process, but so too does reporting very specific fantasies, since the precise organization of these ideas reveals on further analysis a very great deal about the person's relations to his mother and father. Talking about one's fantasies, finding out what they really are, can only take place in an atmosphere of absolute trust, because each person will have a "primitive" belief that he or she will be mercilessly punished by the gods for entertaining—let alone speaking—the monstrous idea.

Unfortunately for the practice of psychoanalysis and for the patient population of the United States, the punitive arm of the other has entered the clinical space. Few patients will feel unconsciously that they can truly speak sexual and aggressive fantasies even if the analyst openly states that he does not comply with mandatory reporting laws and the other intrusions into the clinical space. The deep belief in the patient that the ideas are in themselves evil and should be punished are now echoed in a cultural mentality that agrees that people must be held accountable for thoughts even if they are expressed in a space designed to be free of dire consequence. So a person who suppresses his violent fantasies toward a younger sibling—an urge that is displaced onto symbolic brothers—might unconsciously block such expressions because he is aware of the Tarasoff rule, which obliges the clinician to tell the police about any patient who expresses a violent idea toward someone else. More likely, however, as time passes the origin of such a fear will be less memorable, if ever known, because a Tarasoff mentality can enter the culture and influence those who live in it without anyone knowing quite why the fear of disclosure exists.

But, it might be objected, surely there is latitude for judicious distinction by the clinician between a truly serious violent idea and one that is only a passing thought and no more. This may be true. But no patient who unconsciously considers the expression of a violent idea will have this in mind as an effective reassurance that will enable him to free-associate. Why? Because no one can know what he or she thinks in the clinical situation until after it has been spoken. No one can know therefore that he will not in the passion of the moment state that he is going to kill his sister. This might happen. Who knows? More to the point, however, the individual who is less likely to act on such ideas—the person, for example, who has sufficient guilt to feel an immediate sense of wrong accompanying a murderous impulse—will be unconsciously deterred in his expression of the impulse because of the marriage between his guilt and a punitive mentality in culture that treats aggression with a violent virtuousness.

Absolute confidentiality permits the patient to harm the objects of his internal world and in so doing to express fully in the presence of the analyst the precise nature of his mental conflict. Experienced clinicians are well aware of the remarkable effectiveness of the clinical space as persons who are suffering from destructive impulses know that they must somehow bring their hate for professional help, just as a person suffering an organic complaint must overcome reticence and embarrassment to expose a part of his body to the physician. To bring illness to the psychoanalyst, the patient needs to state his convictions passionately, which might very well mean repeated expressions of horrific violence toward another person—and to bring his attitude toward others into the transference, when for example he subjects the psychoanalyst to exceptionally subtle means of coercion, turning him or her into a figure within the theater of the patient's internal world. So a patient who experienced his mother as a violently punitive figure may consistently provoke the analyst's anxiety, subtly bringing about in the clinician a punitive and harsh frame of mind. In this way the patient transfers into the clinician something the patient has held within his own personality—as the image of his mother—but that the clinician now also holds and must tolerate.

No psychoanalysis can be effective if the patient does not bring his internal objects into the transference by placing them, as it were, into the clinician, who then analyzes the total process and brings consciousness to bear on the patient's mental illness. But in order for this kind of localized violence to take place, the analysand—and the psychoanalyst—must be free to speak and experience the monstrous. However objectionable such mental contents are, it is essential to the patient's therapeutic cure that he speak the monstrous, that he enact it, in order to have it fully articulated. The gruesome paradox of the Tarasoff decision is that in some respects it will have the effect of preventing the truly violent person from seeking professional help and further prevent many a person who was not truly violent—but only full of destructive impulses—

from discussing destructive parts of the personality. Tarasoff will ultimately increase levels of violence in certain individuals. The threat of punishment, however understandable a primitive feeling it is, is a less-effective deterrent of the violent impulse than is professional treatment of these forms of mental conflict.

Precisely because the clinician is working either with mentally ill people or what would pass as fairly ordinary people with mental difficulties, he will be the recipient of the patient's transfer of disturbance. It is one thing to bring oneself to tell a clinician about a fear of death, for example, which the patient finds crippling; it is another matter to bring that fear into the heart of the psychoanalyst who will come to experience it for himself when he is with the patient. By missing appointments following a session of deep depression, by not responding to telephone follow-ups, and by writing a note of extreme despondency, the patient may bring the clinician to fear that the patient is on the verge of committing suicide. The patient thus, among other things, brings this fear into the analyst, who now knows from within his own emotional reality how it feels to be this particular patient. This is an exceedingly complex process with important and subtle fine details that cannot be illustrated here, but patients often act upon the analyst in one way or another to bring about, through the analyst's countertransference, a sense of what the patient is finding difficult to live with.

A sexually impulsive patient, for example, might dress seductively and talk of sexual relations with the analyst, thus provoking in the clinician an erotic state of mind; a hypomanic individual who always removes himself from effective and true engagement with his difficulties may elicit a shallow and bantering relation with the analyst, illustrating for the clinician how it feels from within to maintain a perpetually euphoric defense against inner life; a person who is afraid that others are out to kill him might bring a knife to a session or put a gun on the table and bring about in the clinician a fear that the patient is going to kill him, thus putting into the clinician his own fear of being murdered. A man who is a cheat and yet worried about the psychopathic parts of himself might elect to pay the clinician in cash and also send an expensive gift, and in so doing perhaps tempt the clinician to collude with such cheating—at least in thought if not in action. All of these transferences bring about a state of mind in the clinician that is the result of the patient's prolonged unconscious manipulation. The analyst, in other words, *encourages* the acting in of such disturbed behavior precisely because it is through such enactment that the patient unconsciously represents himself.

Transferring to the other, then, is a crucial part of the necessary freedom of action in a psychoanalysis. But clearly it is also very disturbing to the patient, as this form of expression intensifies the mental disturbance—thus serving to make it clearer to both participants—and it also raises anxieties in both participants about the loosening of conventional forms of behavior. A patient will act upon the analyst in oftentimes quite mad ways. With the borderline patient—perhaps the most common type of disturbed person—there is a genuine uncertainty about the difference between thinking something and doing it. Although this anxiety is part of the borderline patient's mental illness, its presence means that when this patient acts upon the analyst in the transference he will often bring about uncertainty in the clinician's mind about the difference between imagined and real reality. For example, a borderline patient planned for months to kill his wife, telling the analyst in fine detail about how he would kill her and under what circumstances. The clinician knew this patient to be quite deeply frightened of his own violent thoughts. He was on the one hand unusually well behaved and on the other almost confessionally risky; he would do something inappropriate—such as telling a cop that he fancied the cop—in order to get into trouble.

Did this patient really intend to kill his wife? The analyst at first thought this was simply one of the innumerable dares the patient gave to himself, but over time became less certain, eventually reaching the point where he actually thought it might happen. At this point in the clinical relationship, it can be seen that the analyst now shared the patient's mentality; he could not distinguish between a powerful idea and the power of this idea moving

into actuality. What would happen? A deep and per-
vasive anxiety took over, dominating the mind and
making it exceedingly difficult to think. By analyz-
ing what the patient was doing to the analyst, however, he was able both to understand the power of
the patient's anxieties, and the patient also was able
to feel that the clinician had experienced that power
and at the same time to interpret and detoxify the
imagined action, which gradually faded away. In
the end it was quite clear that this patient was ter-
rified of aggression and was certain that if he en-
tertained the violent parts of his personality he
would be torn into pieces. His defense against such
fears had been consistently to act out in a mildly
provocative way that earned him a repeatedly negative response from co-workers and acquaintances.

When the patient knows that the analyst is not
going to punish him for his projective identifications—oftentimes his use of projection to coerce the
analyst quite aggressively into identifying with an
unwanted feeling, impulse, idea, or person—he will
be able to transfer himself fully into the analyst. In
contemporary psychoanalysis this capacity is at the
heart of the cure of the more disturbed parts of the
personality, the parts that cannot really be reached
through free-associative objectification of repressed
ideas but only through the use of the analyst's personality, where the analyst is forced to hold parts
of the patient. This communication, as opposed to
free-associative discourse, is understood unconsciously by the patient to be the only real way of
conveying the self's disturbed parts to the analyst.

Imagine then the effect on any person who enters a psychoanalysis of either knowing in advance or hearing from the clinician that there are certain mental contents and parts of the self that are impermissible in the consulting room. Before those parts are specified the damage is done, for one exclusion signifies the exclusion of everything that is disturbing and communicates to the patient that he or she must keep the disturbed parts of the personality to the self. But the fact that the law has specified forms of sexuality and aggression as the two bogeymen only poisons the dagger already going into the patient's heart. All patients unconsciously fear the danger to the self brought about by sexual ideas and aggressive impulses; this is at the heart of Freudian psychoanalysis. Knowing that the clinician cannot now guarantee absolute confidentiality, that if the patient were to wander into a conviction that he has abused someone, or perhaps been the victim of an abuse, or if he suddenly imagines vividly cutting up his marital partner, then the analyst may have to call the police, only reinforces for all patients the unconscious conviction that the proper result of bad thoughts is punishment. As self-punishment has already been, in any event, the person's unconscious response to disturbing sexual and aggressive contents, the patient's inner law of the talion marries the state's intervention. Together, they defeat any possibility of a free disclosure of thoughts that might allow the analyst and the patient to understand the factors going into their precise construction.

Because of the climate of fear among psychotherapists, we do not know how widespread and
damaging the third-party intrusions have been. But
it does not require a great deal of thought to fore-
see some of the clinical problems that will arise in
the transference. The acting-out adolescent must
surely be tempted to push the analyst's buttons by
boasting of intended acts of harm, manipulating the
clinician into obeying the law but making a fool of
himself and others in the process. It is at such a
moment that some clinicians would ask clarifying
questions, clearly indicating their need to establish
whether the patient is serious. Even if the patient
backs off, he knows he has brought the analyst into
a particular position, one determined by external
factors operating on the clinical relationship. The
child who is angry at not gaining adequate compliance from a child psychotherapist must surely at
times be tempted to bring the clinician to his knees
by inventing an abuse which, if reported, he knows
will compel the clinician into action. The partner
in a marital therapy who feels hard done by in the
therapy and inadequately supported must at times
be tempted to report the other partner as sexually
abusive to her infant, compelling the clinician to
report her to the law. The list of such scenarios is
endless, as varied and precise in enactment as the
patient's own inner worlds. Because the clinician
is now a representative of the police, he becomes
for all patients a different transference object. The
transference to the analyst now includes—in the

ordinary unconscious construction of this other—
a policeman, both for the state and for the insurance company.

That the patient may reckon the analyst does not
particularly like this conscription is at times no
doubt all the more tempting, as the clinician can
be forced into highly difficult situations. As a consequence, those patients who suffer from an excess
of omnipotence, and who are therefore disturbed
by their destructive manipulations of the other, are
now endowed with an actual omnipotence in relation to the analyst.

Already many clinicians state privately that they
do not comply with the law. A patient may report
an abuse, but the clinician considers it either a fantasy or a malicious verbal action that needs time
and analysis to work through. Or a patient says he
intends to kill his boss for a slight, but the analyst
believes that the patient is only expressing his violent ideas and overstating them out of anxiety, not
intention. The analyst waits because he knows his
patient needs to experience his own eventual modu-
lation of the violent ideas, which is much to the
benefit of his own total well-being. But as the population becomes increasingly aware of the clinician's
mandatory obligations, the patient may reckon that
the analyst does not do exactly what he is supposed
to do. Nowhere is this clearer than in the widespread deception that takes place with managed
care reports when the clinician shows his patient a
meaningless report that is intended to elicit contin-

ued funding without disclosing the truth to the third party.

No one is at peace with these acts of deception. While it may be therapeutically useful to an overly compliant patient to see that his analyst is capable of breaking the law or cheating on the filling out of a form, these observations influence the patient's belief in the integrity of his analyst. Even if he may admire the clinician for being courageous and defending psychoanalytical practice against the Salem witch hunt atmosphere of contemporary American culture, he is unwittingly drawn into an unfortunate exploitation of the positive transference as he bonds with his clinician: the analytical couple marries through mutual secrecy and defiance of the state. Either way—admiration or shock—the analyst's behavior has significantly contaminated the transference space, since he has taken and continues to take an action that is exceedingly powerful and definitive. It is at times very difficult for the patient to create an object out of the patient's internal world when the actual other acts so decisively in reality.

While the wish to stop potential or actual crimes against the person is understandable, few have asked what the abrogation of confidentiality has done to the practice of psychotherapy—not to mention whether it actually makes anyone safer. Instead of questions, we have cooperation: clinicians who comply willingly with the reporting laws and other intrusions, graduate schools that teach students how to comply, and judges who, for all their sympathy with the goals of treatment, defer to other social and legal interests, interests at once more familiar and better defined. Reasons for disclosure and exceptions to privilege multiply in the absence of any coherent protest from psychoanalysis or psychotherapy.

It is self evident that as time passes and the public knows more about the destruction of privilege, individuals who might otherwise seek professional help for criminal impulses will not do so. We have also argued that the ordinary patient will, in time, feel inhibited, to lesser and greater degrees, by the knowledge that certain kinds of disclosure will compel a clinician to inform the police. Thus the right to free association is intruded upon by external forces that only compound the resistance that expresses the analysand's moral antipathy toward the destructive sides of the personality. What we have not discussed, however, is the effect of these intrusions on the psychoanalyst's frame of mind.

If free association is difficult to explain to a public that sees psychoanalysis as at best an indulgence and at worse collusive with the illnesses it presumes to treat, then what is termed the psychoanalyst's "neutrality," a feature of his "evenly suspended attentiveness" that permits inner objects to emerge from a kind of internal blank screen will seem even more irksome. But speak up for it one must, as it is this aspect of psychoanalysis that now suffers the greatest damage.

For the last forty years, psychoanalysts in the United States, Europe, and South America have increasingly focused on the clinical significance of the psychoanalyst's countertransference, the shifting inner world of the analyst's thoughts, feelings, and somatic states as he listens in the meditative state of evenly suspended attentiveness.[3] In the countertransference, the analyst receives the patient's unconscious communications at their deepest level—such as dread of loss, which the analyst may well feel before the patient is ever conscious that it forms a part of his own anxieties. This very profound act of reception is unconsciously comprehended by the patient who in turn uses it to express more fully and completely his internal world through his transference. To use his own subjective states as a valued source of clinical material, the analyst must not judge himself harshly for whatever he is thinking. On the contrary, it is now accepted that whatever the mental contents or feelings crossing his mind, they are potentially valuable sources of material that must be respected and stored for potential use and understanding.

Needless to say, the ability to use one's countertransference requires considerable skill and can only be developed after years of training. But the journals of psychotherapy and psychoanalysis re-

3. Perhaps the best introductory text on this subject is *On Learning from the Patient* by Patrick Casement (1985).

flect its significance; no other technical topic has dominated the literature over the last ten years as has countertransference. Interest continues to grow and expand, even into the previously reticent world of classical American psychoanalysis.

The analyst now regards his inner world as a receptive "blank screen" that registers aspects of the patient's communications through the analyst's feelings and mental contents. As he listens to his patient, he develops internal objects derived from work with that particular patient. An inner object such as the patient's mother or brother or boss is built up over time through countless reports and each object is in fact more of a highly complex and multilayered internal state that comes into being each time the patient mentions the object or anytime the object crosses the analyst's mind. Psychoanalysts have increasingly understood the psychic significance of such inner objects and as time passes in work with the patient the clinician gradually analyzes these inner objects, which are in the psychoanalyst, and from such private self-analyses is able to derive important hypotheses about his patient's inner life and personal relationships.

It will come as no surprise that for the analyst to constitute such a blank screen or to be receptive to the patient's communications, there can be no serious extraneous contamination of this psychic structure and process. It is a tool—like a musical

instrument—that must be protected if it is to function. It can be displaced and made inoperative, and
when this occurs the clinician can no longer function psychoanalytically. As his expertise is the provision of psychoanalysis, cessation of the capacity
to function psychoanalytically is a serious matter
of concern.

Unfortunately, the incursion into clinical space
of third-party interests now means that the practicing psychoanalyst's blank screen is littered with
legal scriptures that demand various forms of compliance. As he listens to certain sexual disclosures,
what appears on the screen is not the unconscious
significations of such mental contents but the flash-
ing red lights of the police car that may have to be
called to the door. So, too, with aggressive contents;
during some reports the analyst will find himself
gazing not at the patient's inner world but at the
Tarasoff patrol. Similarly, listening to a maritally
estranged person, he is jostled by the realization
that he may be called to testify in court. The same
is true for a patient litigating an alleged sexual
harassment in the workplace. Even if he knows that
his patient's comments are so comparatively in-
nocuous as to be legitimately outside the law, the
psychic effect is the same: the screen of receptive
listening no longer exists. In turn, the capacity to
receive the patient's communications from an attitude of evenly suspended attentiveness—when the
analyst drifts along in his own world of associative
thought and feeling—is also destroyed as the clini-

cian will bear an increasingly menacing internal object: the heavy footsteps of the state.

A child psychotherapist has agreed to see a 7-year-old boy who is school phobic and deathly afraid of cars. The child is profoundly attached to his mother and in the third session makes up a story about what a monster his father is. At the verge of this exceedingly important point of unconscious communication the analyst is no longer able to think freely. In the back of his mind is a consistent and unremitting dread that this child is going to report an abuse and subject the clinician to an impossible conflict of interests. Unable to restore neutrality he privately mourns the loss of his professional capacity with this young boy whom he knows he is failing by his own inner anxiety.

A female psychotherapist sees a young man of 22 in psychotherapy. It is clear from his hesitations and embarrassment that he is struggling with sexual feelings toward the clinician, but in a few weeks' time he moves from these sexual states into a pathologic resolution: he tells the clinician that he is attracted to a woman who lives across the street and is going to rape her. He describes his rape fantasy in great detail. Even though the clinician can see that he is aiming to provoke her, she is unable to maintain a receptive area within herself because she is increasingly troubled, knowing that she is on the border of having to report the patient to the local authorities; his comments threaten a harmful act.

An experienced analyst sees a borderline female patient for a consultation. She says she wants an analysis. After fifteen minutes, the patient reports that she was consistently raped by her father over fifteen years of her life and she has told her sisters and mother. She wants help to confront the father and believes that by prosecuting him she can at last overcome her blind refusal to take her own life into her hands. The analyst does not know if her allegation is true or not. He does know, however, that he cannot now conduct a psychoanalysis. For whether or not the patient is telling the truth, he is aware that the presence of the mandatory reporting laws, and the possibility of civil or criminal liability if he does not accept her account as factual, mean that he will not be able to construct a blank screen for this patient that would enable him to offer her a true psychoanalysis.

As intrusive as the reporting laws are, the average clinician might well point to the more immediately distressing effects of managed care supervision of work with a patient. Increasingly, managed care providers not only are opting for shorter treatment and for medication over psychotherapy, but they are also actively opposing long-term psychotherapy or psychoanalysis. Indeed, some companies target the patient's "dependence" on the analyst as a contraindication of further coverage. Thus clinicians, oddly enough, find themselves fearing therapeutic success, since with many patients it is precisely the capacity to depend upon the analyst that ultimately insures a greater degree of personal autonomy for the patient.[4]

In psychiatric residency programs, graduate schools of psychology, schools of social work, and increasingly in the professional literature, psychotherapists are being urged to cooperate with the plethora of purportedly reasonable intrusions into privilege.[5] A major aspect of such cooperation is clinical note taking. So many clinicians have had their notes subpoenaed that professionals are now advised to take careful notes of their sessions so as to have something to provide if a subpoena arrives. In some states, professional licensing bodies have identified the failure to take adequate notes as evi-

---

4. For a complete discussion of these issues and a concise analysis of the effects of managed care on the practice of psychotherapy, see Miller (1994) a booklet that may be ordered from Boulder Psychotherapists' Press, Inc., 350 Broadway, Suite 210, Boulder, CO 80303.

5. Thus Brunner/Mazel joins a publishing bandwagon as they promote a new book, *The Preferred Provider's Handbook* by William L. Poynter (1994). Under the banner "Managed Care is Coming" the prepublication flyer announces that "while your colleagues worry about what the future will bring . . . you'll be reading . . . and learning how to *survive and thrive* in your private practice." The aim of the book is to help "psychotherapists gain an intellectual understanding and psychological acceptance of this often unwelcome new system. It is only when they 'come to terms' with managed care that practitioners will be able to make the system work for them." See also Kalichman (1993), which offers an elaborate rationale for compliance with the reporting laws.

dence of lack of professionalism by the clinician. Newcomers are taught how to write notes to managed care conglomerates, and to accommodate the fact that the reader is often not a clinician, but a clerk—a clerk who will decide whether treatment can continue or not. The litigious spirit of contemporary American society is such that therapists may take notes simply because they know that patients in a negative transference will take them to court.

For whom, however, are such notes kept?

In the past, psychoanalysts retained an intriguing system of notation. Few had either the time or the inclination to keep process notes, a fairly complete account of the full course of a session, unless they wished to record the history of the analysis or were preparing a clinical presentation to colleagues. Most simply noted occasional dreams of the patient, significant mental events, and their own musings. As an analysis takes from four to six years, although such notes were by no means exhaustive, in time they became a kind of stream of consciousness—the analyst's *Ulysses*—that shadowed the treatment. On rare but important occasions the analyst might review these notes, usually when he felt stuck in working with the patient, and the spirit of its medium (casual, pensive, punctuational, associative) was as essential to his rethinkings as any of its specific contents. Such notes were his own private diary and even if rarely consulted satisfied his need for some unintrusive other who would carry the analysis and with whom he could consult, some other who would know but never intrude.

One of the most influential postwar psychoanalysts, Wilfred Bion, wrote that each psychoanalyst should approach his analysand before a session "without memory or desire." Psychoanalysts who have never read Bion know this phrase. It captures something that all analysts know and in differing ways do; before the session they create that inner blank screen by relaxing into a suspended state of mind, one removed from memories of the previous hour, one divorced from a desire to work on any particular issue with the patient. Why? So that the patient might once again enjoy the essential privilege of a space that receives him without prejudgment. He is free in this space. He can say anything he wishes and it will be out of his immediate discourse that the analyst will derive his own inner cogitations.

The analyst's notes of this interesting journey are loose and sketchy so that at a glance they facilitate his associations without becoming part of a formative agenda. Yet into the loosely associative world of the analyst's diary now intrudes a demand for a coherent organized account of the progress of sessions that is simply a lie. Analysts must now falsify the very nature of their work so that those who should not be intruding into this confidential relationship might be able to read about it in terms comprehensible to them. The analyst is now writing for the state and to the state.[6]

Another intrusion on the psychoanalytic process appeared recently when a psychoanalyst presented a case to a visiting colleague at a small conference. In the course of describing the patient's capacity to delude herself the presenter indicated that she had suffered from a conviction that she had molested her child. Some time was devoted to deconstructing this conviction, which, among other matters, led to a realization that the patient did not even know terms for the parts of the body or what she meant by molested. It became clear that she suffered intense anxieties of a sexual kind that led to wide-ranging delusions. No sooner had the analyst presented the case when a conference participant asked if the presenter had reported this alleged abuse to the local authorities. The letter of the law as it is written requires such reporting. The ques-

---

6. The code of conduct of the American Psychological Association ordains that the psychologist conceive of himself, when writing notes, as a potential informant, who must therefore write up sessions with disclosure in mind. Section 1.23(b), "Documentation of Professional and Scientific Work," says, "When psychologists have reason to believe that records of their professional services will be used in legal proceedings involving recipients of or participants in their work, they have a responsibility to create and maintain documentation *in the kind of detail and quality that would be consistent with reasonable scrutiny in an adjudicative forum"* (p. xxxviii, italics added).

tioner continued with the point and accused the analyst of negligence. The atmosphere in the room changed immediately from a considerate assessment of the nature of the hysterical process in a patient to, in effect, an emotional debate about the right to speak freely about that process.

Doubtless few in the room realized the consequence of discussing the delusional patient in light of the reporting laws. But no one who left the conference that day was in any doubt about the destructive effects of the law as it exists. Such a law does not allow for clinical judgment; it does not give adequate discretion to the clinician to determine the difference between delusional states of mind and lucid reports of an abuse. Thus at the very time that psychoanalysts should be conferring on the vital distinctions—albeit hard to come by—between hysterical delusions and perverse personalities, the possibility of an open forum is increasingly remote. As long as the laws, regulatory agencies, and the press demand reporting, then any clinician presenting a patient who believed he had committed a sexually aggressive act would have to report to the police in order to avoid bringing himself and his audience into immediate conflict with the law.

Although it is our view that psychoanalysts should not be deterred by this hazard, it will surely make many reluctant to bring their work—with certain patients, at least—into conference forums. Thus the hysterical and the paranoid analysands, the schizophrenic, the borderline personality, all of whom develop delusions surrounding their sexual and aggressive lives, will suffer from the intimidation and the diminished intellectual resources of the analysts they rely on for treatment.

How seriously will those resources be diminished? The individual who chastised the presenting analyst at the conference we described in effect reported her, and the conferees had an immediate experience of the intimidating effect of thought police. One of the authors of this study worked in Poland and Hungary before the fall of the Soviet-backed regimes, when psychoanalysis was still more or less underground. The current feeling among American clinicians about the invasion of what should be a private relationship reminds him of supervisory work with Eastern European analysts who worked in fear of state intervention.

Some might find this analogy exaggerated and unduly alarmist. Even in Eastern Europe, after all, comparatively few people were ever arrested and imprisoned, and very few psychoanalysts and psychotherapists are now prosecuted by the authorities. How can a small amount of worry be so destructive? It might not be in other professions. If a bookbinder is afraid of arbitrary state intervention in his life, the fear may not directly effect his binding of books. A dentist's hand may tremble a bit from equivalent anxieties, but even so, he may be able to block them off and perform his duties. But the psychoanalyst relies upon the psychic inner freedom of his own mind in order to receive his analysand fully and properly. If he is distracted, he and his patient cannot create psychoanalysis. Analysts in Eastern Europe were not meant to exist in the first place, but few were ever incarcerated for doing so. Nonetheless, the danger intervened and diminished their capacity to be fully receptive to patients; something of the illness of culture afflicted both participants in the analytic process. So, too, in contemporary American culture has the modern clinician been afflicted by a misguided zeal that demands that clinicians become an arm of state intervention. Psychoanalysts and their patients cannot now form that inner psychic space that is essential to the creation of a psychoanalysis. Without that space, the form of treatment that has carefully evolved for over one hundred years cannot exist.

As managed care providers now demand regular reports on those in treatment, we are witness to a more insidious invasion of the psychoanalytical space than was possible to envision some twenty years ago. Who was to know that the provider's interest in cost-effectiveness would corrupt peer review, as "evaluators" with no clinical training took charge, putting the corporation's needs—for as little payout as possible—ahead of a patient's clinical requirements? Was it foreseeable that large pharmaceutical companies would purchase managed care institutions, thus ordaining the use of psychotropic interventions to their own further profit?[7] Even though medications are often an important part of individual treatment, no drug in and of itself consistently resolves human pain and conflict. The health care industry, however, looks for the quick fix: a worker ready to go back on the job and no longer a burden to the company funds. Those analysts who do not agree to write reports on insured patients are dropped and blacklisted. Colleagues who continue to work within this environment are afraid to speak out against providers who often write in a gag rule for their employees: criticize the company and what is going on and you are out of a job.

The transformation of psychoanalysis from a specialized treatment with unique features in its curative process to a cost-effective unit that must continually report on its progress toward symptom elimination has gravely affected the frames of mind of any analyst or patient still participating in such an environment. It is not only that patients are often distressed at the forced disclosure of what is taking place in the treatment, at the fact that the most private, disturbed communications may have to be described in order to justify further care, at the fact

---

7. Walls (1994) cites reports in the *New York Times* of Ely Lilly & Company's announcement that it was buying the PCS Health System, the largest manager of drug benefit programs in the United States. Two other giant corporations—Smith-Kline-Beecham and Merck and Company (the largest manufacturer of drugs in the world) have recently acquired managed care networks.

that such disclosures are often deeply embarrassing and natural deterrents to further free disclosures of what is taking place inside the self. It is not only that both participants are concerned about the potential fate of private details, which could go to the employer or into a national data bank. What destroys the ecosystem of psychoanalysis is the health industry mentality that regards mental illness and human suffering as an enemy village to be taken out with surgical strikes as quickly and cleanly as possible. It is ultimately the awareness that human life is marketed and controlled by these companies that destroys the psychoanalytical frame of mind. Psychoanalysis has always viewed human conflict as not only inevitable but essential; a mind in conflict is evidence of the enlivened engagement of any self with its world. Such a mind is not to be medicated into subemotive and conflict-free functioning. It is not an enemy. Excess mental conflict—of the sort that creates symptoms—needs analytical understanding and treatment to restore the mind to ordinary conflict. The meanings expressed in intense conflicted suffering are as profound as the soul itself; analysis restores to the individual what he or she means through the constellation of symptoms.

Certain persons—borderline or narcissistic—may have suffered such early mental deprivation that they cannot conjure symptomatic conflict; they are less able to symbolize their unconscious life. Because of anxieties that were too severe in rela-

tion to the mother and the father, such people do
not have the benefits normally present in family life,
such as the benefit of generative conflict between
self and family members that assists in the definition of one's own personality. Psychoanalytical
work aims in part to bring these individuals into
an intimate relation with the other—the transference—which evokes thoughts and feelings that put
the patients in useful conflict—first, with the psychoanalyst and in time with themselves. What
might initially feel like the analyst's ill-tempered
thoughtlessness eventually comes to be understood
as the patients' projection of a dismissive portion
of their own personality. Once these defenses are
worked through, then the analysand can more
clearly objectify those other conflicts that arise
from a life and that more distinctly register the
person's idiom.

Psychoanalysis encourages the evolution of certain mental conflicts, a process that among other
things takes time, and resolves the destructive sides
of such conflict not by suppressing knowledge of
them (as with medication) but by increasing insight
into them. In this way, the positive sides of conflict—that each symptom and each character disorder contains within it the autobiography of an
individual self—are preserved and valued while
their toxic effect is mitigated.

Those who aim to minimize the irksome chal-
lenges of the conflicting other are unlikely to be in
sympathy with the perspective of psychoanalysis.

And while those working in pharmaceuticals and advocating the wider use of drugs do so for honorable reasons, they now operate within a system that uses these products to suppress the conflictual sides of an entire population. Further, the health industry complex—drug companies and their hospital care systems—are now targeting psychoanalysis as the enemy; what they disparagingly call the "New Yorker syndrome" (Henneberger 1994). This contempt for a self that presumably seeks psychoanalysis in order to transform psychological disturbance into manageable meaning, a self that may indeed come to see this form of insight as pleasurable, shows up in the assault on the features of psychoanalysis: its consumption of time, its valuation of talking as opposed to doing, its lack of programmatic direction, its freedoms of the mind. Is it not ironic that a country deeply alarmed by the consumption of illegal drugs should nonetheless utterly fail to see the link between its national ingestion disorder and the hatred of talking freely? How like the adolescent—who just wants to act out by taking a drug to destroy disturbing meanings in a life— the health industry complex has become. That this mentality should seriously erode a psychoanalysis if confidentiality is invaded, as it has been, is not surprising, and the cause of these developments is the subject of our next chapter. Perhaps we may introduce it by extending our discussion in a political direction.

The health industry complex is part of a culture

willing to subdue discourse through the miracles of modern chemistry. Part of the industry supports the publication of scientific research that inevitably finds some underlying biological or organic cause of any mental state. However, this paradigm is applicable only to the individual in distress. Would a marital therapist assessing a problem recommend Zoloft to the husband and Anafranil to the wife? If eight people in group psychotherapy develop an irrational hate toward one of the group members, should they all neutralize it with Xanax? Have they all joined in a biological synchronicity, suffering the same chemically driven disorder at the same time? Should we develop a medication for anti-Semitism? Even when medication helps, it is seldom a solution for these kinds of problems that need to be opened up by talking and by the subversive (not suppressive) effect of speech. Suppression is part of the problem, not a part of any liberated solution.

As a political act, similarly, psychoanalysis offers freedom through the democratic function of free speech. Just as all sides of a group conflict have a voice if such freedom to speak is encouraged, talking freely represents all sides of a single personality, a kind of parliament of all the desires, demands, anxieties, and identifications of any self. Medication all too often suppresses representation. That is why when it works it works quite well: it effectively silences a self or at least troublesome or disruptive aspects of it.

The Zolofts and Xanaxes, the new gods of our culture, have permitted micro-acts of political oppression, as that which should be heard in a person, in that parliament of speech that is a psychoanalysis, is foreclosed. The underlying hatred of relationships—one reason that many people turn in bitter despair to the self-stimulating, cocooned universe of illegal drugs—is also utilized by the managed care companies, which, interestingly enough, also view emotional and psychological growth through relationships, long-term psychotherapy in particular, with thinly concealed hate (Miller 1994). With medication, once again an entire culture turns to the solitary and destructive— even if legal—solution of chemical ingestion as an alternative to participatory growth through understanding and engaged relating. The unwitting but telling aim of the health industry complex is to suppress individual freedom and to create a nation of "normopaths" or "normotics"[8]—the abnormally normal—for whom psychological conflict is viewed at worse as endangering or, at least, as vulgar. In the end, such anxieties reflect a fear and loathing of freedom itself.

---

8. The first psychoanalyst to write in depth about a certain type of intention in a person—a defensive movement toward an extreme in normality—was Joyce McDougall (1980). She defined this person as a *normopath*. A different emphasis, using another, less-effective term, *the normotic* is to be found in Bollas (1987).

4

CREATING INFORMANTS

It is undeniably hazardous to consider why psychoanalysis has lost the privilege of confidentiality, since the historical process is still taking place. It is useful, however, to reflect on certain trends so as to consider in the next chapter what steps could be taken to restore what has been taken away. We have already suggested a few important developments.

The widespread social alarm created by the work of the Kempes in the early 1960s shocked a nation that, until that time, had assumed that child abuse was negligible. There was at first sight little that could be done about what was described as an epidemic. The cost to states and county governments of training a new generation of child abuse investigators would have been great. A population in panic needed a swift response. Deputizing thousands of psychotherapists as mandatory informants was in some respects an ingenious solution; therapists were on the front lines, working with individuals and families in trouble. Few at the time considered the long-term effect on psychotherapy of this newly assigned role.

From sexual abuse sprang interest in physically abused children, which in turn broadened to psychological abuse. The concept of psychological abuse expanded from the child who was a clear victim of deliberate and sadistic parental torment to persons who suffered as a consequence of their parents' personalities; thus, there were victims of parents who were alcoholics, gamblers, multiple movers, workaholics, and the like. All that was needed, it seemed, was a clear identification of an abusive action or situation and the victim could claim a right to action.

Who was to know, furthermore, that the abused child would evoke powerful and deep senses of identification, so that in viewing the abused child, tens of thousands of Americans also saw the hidden abused child within the self. Why such deep and intense identification with a neglected child? Perhaps this powerful sense of ubiquitous harm derives in part from a mass social decision to abandon children to empty homes, from the creation of the latchkey child who has lost his parents to their professional and economic necessities. Across America, forlorn pictures of "missing" children gazed from milk cartons at children who were themselves all too often lost souls. In addition to the sad reality of those children who were truly missing, either runaways or kidnapped, were thousands of others who drank that milk at an empty table.

Earlier, the country sent its young men to senseless deaths in Vietnam, creating vacant spaces in homes across the nation, now missing a son or a brother or a father. Then the country would be obsessed with those missing in action—the MIAs—blaming the Vietnamese for holding them in concentration camps. Was this preoccupation with the MIAs about the enemy that took them and refused to give them back? Or about the country that sent them to an appallingly meaningless death? To grieve properly for that profound loss, however, the nation would have to acknowledge why the MIAs were missing in the first place, but guilt over a meaningless and vicious war foreclosed true grief. That guilt was displaced onto the MIAs who would be missing forever and yet remain as a potentially retrievable other if the enemy would only give them back.

To be able to do something about recovering or restoring the missing self became something of an unconscious national obsession. By identification with victims anywhere—the child, the abused woman, the spouse of an alcoholic—actions could be taken to put things right. Through a curious marriage with therapy and therapists, Americans discovered the hidden child within. Therapy could teach them that this child had been missing because of abuse and could now be found, loved, and nurtured back into reality. It was not an uncommon fact of family life for real children to find themselves taking a backseat to the rediscovered child in the parent.

Self-realization was not new to American therapeutic culture. In the period immediately preceding the Kempes revolution and throughout the 1960s, scores of encounter therapies, primal therapies, and self-actualization methods were available to increasing numbers of people who, in a version of the fast-food culture, actually felt altered by a long weekend of clinical work. To provide the feeling of such change quickly, therapists needed a shorthand language and a model that anyone could use, and the family was the handiest model of its kind. Thus someone in group or individual therapy would be the father, someone the mother, and someone the child who would then speak hidden— usually hurt and angry—feelings to a failing parent. The stage was set for a play that would run in countless theatres across the United States. Alas, for every truth contained in such hurt feelings was a countertruth, that very often the destructive feature of the parent was in fact a projection of a disturbing part of the plaintiff's personality. Thus as blame was put into the parents, the destructive sides of the personality were removed from self-awareness. In time, these therapies gradually assisted the individual to lose contact with the troubled and troubling sides of the self. Psychoanalysis, with its more cumbersome and tedious method of work, with its irksome emphasis on the subject's desire and destructiveness, seemed deeply unsympathetic to the tenor of the times, to the need to create political objects of corrective vilification.

One of the reasons that the mental health professions not only failed to resist the loss of their privileged relation to their clients but actually assisted in its dismantling is the belief that the patient should objectify the cause of emotional harm—the inadequate parent—and then proceed to take verbal action. Indeed, many therapists actively encouraged their patients to come to the point where they could "trust their feelings." At an opportune time the "perp"—the mother or father—was invited into the consulting room where the patient in the presence of the therapist would articulate his or her hurt. For the parent who attended, this was often a deeply disturbing and confusing occasion. A refusal to attend amounted to an admission of guilt that permitted a judgment in absentia.

Thus breaches of confidentiality were actively sought by both therapist and patient; both searched for others who would have to listen to their conclusions. While in the psychoanalytic relationship every patient was encouraged to maintain the privacy of what was disclosed, especially during periods of intense hate toward a critical figure, in many therapies the opposite was the rule. If an analysand told a friend about what was happening in his or her analysis, the analyst would take this up upon its reporting and indicate how doing so, however gratifying and reassuring, diluted the professional couple's capacity to process those feelings, memories, and ideas that were emerging at the time. A client in therapy, however, who reported the same sort of disclosure would be encouraged to do so; this was evidence of increased empowerment and a newfound courage to tell the world about the self. Friends became co-confidants to therapists.

In the early l960s there were hundreds of different types of "therapy" offered by individuals from numerous schools of thought. For very good reasons, the state legislatures moved toward the licensing of psychotherapists, demanding credentials that required a qualified training, the passing of an examination, and licensure by a state board of examiners. By the early l970s there was something of a stampede by counselors and therapists into programs where they could obtain the needed credentials. Further, while clinical psychology had been the poor sibling to academic psychology throughout the century, suddenly schools of psychology were inundated by people who wanted clinical training in order to gain certification. Schools of social work became places for people who actually had no intention of doing social work but found it the only way to practice psychotherapy with a license that was not too difficult to get. New trainings and licenses were created, such as the Marriage and Family Counselor in California, that were hybrids of prior degree programs. By the end of the 1970s, the number of qualified mental health professionals had increased many times over.

We need to keep in mind that one important aspect of this licensing rush was a need to satisfy the statutory requirements set by the state. It is intriguing that the diversity and fecund therapeutic inventiveness of the early 1960s yielded to armies of MFCCs, Ph.D.s, and L.C.S.W.s who marched with remarkable skill and speed through their trainings. We believe that one important aspect of this transformation was an identification with state-sanctioned respectability, perhaps further galvanized by prior states of rebelliousness toward that same state. The fact that such professionalization of psychotherapy was right and long overdue only fed the sense of a righteous advance. And while the textures of righteousness are exceedingly complex in contemporary America, two interesting strands are the professionalization of once-radical therapists and the legislatively inspired hunt for villains who had abused children.

A generation that took on the misguided judgments of its parental guardians about Vietnam would find it easy to identify with the victim of child abuse and would also feel disinclined to keep its revelations bounded by clinical space. The disclosing self in any event is an important part of Ameri-

can culture, from Wigglesworth, Melville, and
Whitman, to Hemingway, Mailer, and confessional
poets like Robert Lowell, Sylvia Plath, and Anne
Sexton (not to mention its vulgarized appearances
on network television). In America, the self in-
fringed upon by any factor that removes an important right is also a publicly disclosing self. We do
not suggest, however, that identification with victims of abuse was by any means consciously developed by the newly licensed therapists. We believe
there was an unconscious evolution that had important outcomes—some good, such as increased
vigilance for neglected children, and some bad,
such as the elimination of confidentiality from
clinical practice.

Indeed, we may wonder how many psychotherapists actually believed in privilege or knew about
it in the first place. As we have maintained, the
encounter cultures were highly disclosing and
hardly dedicated to working matters through in
private. We have also suggested that identification
with state-sanctioned professionalism led many to
identify with the state's interests, and by warning
the state of misdeeds done, some therapists were
continuing a 1960s tradition of turning to the world
to seek redress against villains. But by the mid-1980s
a certain irony appears in all these developments.

A small child who is molested has lost a fundamental right that all children should enjoy: the right
to love a parent and receive love in return that is
not a sexual violation. He or she also has the right

to bodily and psychic privacy. Sexual molestation of the child removes these rights and does so in such a traumatizing way that the child loses his sense that they ever existed. Is it not ironic that the psychotherapist now suffers a corresponding loss? Surely there is unconscious interest—for patients, for therapists, and for the public—in such an exchange, in the fact that psychotherapists had lost a fundamental right so completely that any sense of its sanctity is gone as well. By the 1980s many a therapist knew all too well from experience about this loss but had no language to express it, no sense of how it came to be, and no remedy from colleagues or from the surrounding culture.

The depth of the unconscious identification by patients with the missed child who must not be left and must be saved (recall that this was the generation raised in the ambience of the absent father) continued to influence the way that clinicians managed their clients. In the psychoanalytic setting the analyst had usually maintained quite clear boundaries on behalf of his patient. What was disturbing the patient should be disclosed in sessions. These sessions were usually three to five times a week, sufficient time for a thorough response to anxieties and regressions, so that the patient's effort to expand the boundaries of coverage—to telephone calls, extra sessions, weekend visits, and forms of practical assistance—could be interpreted in terms of what was taking place at that time in the analysis. But in the mentality of victimhood, a deprived patient who telephoned the clinician required and produced what we might term "beeper therapy." Clinicians rushed from dining tables, movie theatres, and vacation beaches to the telephone because one of their patients wanted to chat on the phone. Such provision of care was no doubt tiresome, but in the sweeping fashions of therapy world, it became *de rigueur*. By the late 1980s the abused patient had now evolved into the multiple patient with so many selves that therapists were accustomed to the idea that the self who appeared in the consulting room was not the self on the phone, and so there were different forums of treatment for the different parts of each self.

By this expanded presence in their patient's lives, many therapists unwittingly assumed an omnipotent position. For each and every psychic pain there was a telephone link and a beeper or a telephone answering machine giving numbers where the clinician could be reached at any time. How does this development bear on the loss of privilege? In our view it resulted first in an implicit license: the therapist assumed a disproportionate authority to affect the patient's external life on a day-to-day basis, thus bringing clinical work out of the consulting room and into the everyday spaces of experience. This extension of the ambition and claim of psychotherapy, from analysis of internal worlds to strategic intervention in the actual world, led to therapists who involved third persons in the therapy. From here it was not a long step for therapists to appear in court—initially, at least, on their patient's behalf.

In our experience, few therapists of this generation were pleased to appear in court, whether in a custody battle or in a claim against an insurance company or against another litigant. However, when such an appearance seemed to satisfy the essential need of the client for empowerment, it often seemed the right thing to do. And many of their colleagues had preceded them to the courtroom. For decades, prosecution and defense attorneys had used mental health professionals as expert witnesses, brought into the court to discuss an assessment reached most often in a private consultation. Anglo-American criminal law requires proof beyond a reasonable doubt of *mens rea*, a culpable mental state such as malice aforethought or premeditation. It is understandable, therefore, why attorneys would want to engage a psychiatrist or psychologist to provide expert testimony, either to prosecute someone for being sane at the time or to gain a lesser charge for a client suffering from diminished mental capacity. However, in their compliance with these requests expert witnesses did not give attention to the long-term outcome. For although they would sometimes not disclose actual statements made to them in confidence by the interviewee, their agreement to disclose a diagnostic opinion to the courts was an ethical violation of the obligation to preserve confidence. In the end, expert witnesses have not gained public credibility, because for each witness for the prosecution, another equally convincing one can be found for the defense, each claiming an expertise that in the world of mental health few could ever legitimately claim except in the most tangential and problematic manner. Who can know what was in the mind of a person who commits a violent crime at the time it took place?

Forensic psychiatry is a creature of the 1970s, emerging in Great Britain and the United States under social pressure for action against mentally deranged criminals. The subspecialty blossomed, ironically enough, as the hospitals emptied their patients into the streets. Many of them would subsequently be processed in the courts, where they would at last meet up with a psychiatrist or psychologist, although now in a different role: a functionary of the state, rather than a healer of the mentally disturbed. Although psychologists, social workers, and psychiatrists working within the prison service and in other specialized treatment locations for the criminally inclined perform a valued service, an important line was crossed when such professionals agreed to represent the court or council as expert witnesses.

It is part of their assigned professional task to violate confidentiality, and, although in the literature they are careful to point out that they do not guarantee confidentiality, at no point do they raise the more troubling issue that many of the people who consent to discuss their states of mind with a psychiatrist, psychologist, or social worker will unconsciously feel that it is safe to do so and will not result in a disclosure of what they reveal. And while it is regrettably true that in a sense forensic workers have indeed gained a certain expertise in the interface between law and psychotherapy, psychotherapists and psychoanalysts should not see such violations of confidentiality as vanguard actions, but as the profound breaches of trust that they are. Even if the mental health profession finds a publicly useful distinction between those who would work as social therapists and those who would offer clinical sessions as private psychotherapists—an issue we discuss at greater length in the next chapter—it nonetheless remains a matter of serious ethical concern that the state should ever delegate a member of the mental health professions to conduct an interview whose contents are then disclosed in a setting where the finding of guilt or innocence, the custody or loss of children, or the length of a sentence would depend in part on these disclosures.

We now find, furthermore, that psychiatrists and psychologists—acting on behalf of the court— make a diagnostic assessment and a judicial decision at the same time. A Royal College of Psychiatry handbook—*Child Psychiatry and the Law*—tells us that "a child psychiatrist's opinion may be sought when a child's development or behavior is abnormal and the court wants to know to what extent parental practices are responsible for the situation"

(p. 31). Thus the forensic worker is called upon to make a judgment about the suitability of the parents. We find this same handbook further blurring the boundary between disclosure, assessment, and judgment. It tells us that parents being assessed "should at the very least feel that they have had an open-minded, sympathetic hearing" from the psychiatrist, thus tellingly indicating how the psychiatrist should use his clinical skill to lull the parent into the false assumption that this is indeed a place where one may confide in an ethical other. "If at the time of seeing the parents the psychiatrist knows what his or her final conclusion will be" the handbook continues "it is good practice to tell the parents this, and explain the reasons for it" (p. 22). Here there is no meaningful distinction between conclusion and judgment and mental health professionals have ventured into a blurring of role that already has deeply disturbing implications for the rights of the individual.

This discussion assumes that psychiatrists and psychologists would agree on the issue of privilege, but we know this is not the case. Both professions are divided over whether or not the patient–therapist relationship is confidential or whether there are exceptions to this rule. Our intent is not to rehearse this debate in its entirety but rather to see what role it plays in the recent abandonment of privilege by the profession.

Nineteenth-century psychiatry viewed many psychological problems as indications of moral degeneration and devised many treatment methods aimed at restoring the moral integrity of the self, which would in turn cure the subject. Some of the most enlightened mental hospitals in the United States saw therapy as a comprehensive process of resurrection through talking, work, healthy leisure, community relations, and the like. It is interesting to see how European psychoanalysis, once it gained admittance in American medical schools, acquired a particularly American interest in adaptation, development, and progress. The most influential post-Freudian book in American medical psychoanalysis, Heinz Hartmann's *The Ego and the Problem of Adaptation* (1958), focused not on the unconscious subject who places his inner life in dreams, symptoms, and parapraxes, but on the developing ego and how it overcomes or suffers difficulties on its integrative path toward increased mastery. The problem of how to master one's world in light of the anxieties each person faces in the course of the life cycle was the subject of the next most influential work in American psychoanalysis, Erik Erikson's *Childhood and Society* (1950), and although Erikson sensitively represented many of the ambiguities of a human life, he was nonetheless an ego psychologist in the Hartmann tradition and, like other psychoanalysts, considered how the patient was doing in adaptation to the norms of behavior in American society.

We bring this short history of psychoanalytic preoccupations to the reader's attention because we believe that without reviewing this outward-bound trend in psychoanalysis, in which a patient's psychic change is measured in terms of his progressive adaptation to the outside world, it is difficult to understand how certain of its features at the time supported disclosure. Analysts and their patients were proud of the signs of increased adaptation. A patient was less anxious and more able to work or less depressed and more able to take pleasure. One patient had resolved identity issues and could marry, while another had children and rose in his profession.

This belief in the outwardly adaptive self as a good sign—not the only one, but an important indicator of the success of psychoanalysis—was itself part of the culture of evidentiary desire. The wishes of nineteenth-century psychiatry that the self indicate moral integration seemed fulfilled, in the different language and models of the twentieth-century analyst, through the more integrated and progressively accomplished individual. Thus, a self that was disabled became a sign of something else—for an ambitious analyst, a sign that his technique was not working or that he was not as good as his colleague down the block, who seemed to have more success with *his* patients. In subtle ways analysts and those they trained in psychology, social work, and other mental health fields became more and more concerned with the adaptive or maladaptive behaviors of their patients. They may have communicated this concern in the form of an anxiety to their patients, who, compared to European and South American patients, are unusually demanding of their clinicians. In turn, the American therapist is often likely to resort to medication to keep the patient on a good behavioral track, even if the depressions or anxieties the patient experiences are psychically essential to an adequate analytical engagement.

However, good behavior by itself is not the only feature of American therapeutic culture. Indeed, the goal of therapy seems to have shifted from the integrated and therefore bolder and more adaptive self of the 1950s to the resurrected and redeemed self of the 1980s and 1990s, and the enterprise now seems at once more reflexive and more evangelical. American bookstores contain scores of books written by patients and former patients about how therapy brought them new life. Instead of learning how to get on the corporate board of directors without undue anxiety, we hear about productive months spent at the Betty Ford Center, where writing is itself an important part of the redemptive process. We believe that there is a significant connection between this atmosphere and the erosion of privilege. Who would want to keep his salvation secret, after all? What better way to spread the good news than to go into print?

We must also consider the view that psychoanalysts themselves, in their clinical writings, were occasionally compromising the patient's sense of confidentiality. Given how removed from public view psychoanalytic journals were, published clinical

work was for a long time read only by fellow analysts. But from the mid-1960s, when intellectual
and academic interest in psychoanalyis grew, the
journals were often perused by scholars and lay-
people. Since the development of that wider interest in psychoanalysis, clinicians have taken differing positions on how best to write about a patient
without a breach of confidentiality. Some analysts
create composite patients, combining aspects of
several patients into one. Others who regard this
as unacceptable disclose the main features of an
analysis while disguising the patient. Some analysts
ask their patients' permission for publication. Still
others, particularly those writing about inner processes that reveal the analyst's ongoing frame of
mind, argue that asking a patient to read such
material is too overwhelming; they maintain that
analysts must be able to write about what goes on
within themselves, and that disguising the patient
is enough. While we discuss measures that can be
taken to address this issue in the next chapter, it is
pertinent to point out that the writing of psychoanalysis is part of the culture of disclosure and not
without its problems.

Disclosing what has gone on in another person's
analysis, either without that person's permission or
because it could not be gained, is an altogether different matter, vividly raised by the controversy over
the Middlebrook book (see Chapter 1). In that case
a biographer gained access to confidential information and published material from sessions, some-

thing agreed upon by the psychiatrist who treated Anne Sexton. Does confidentiality cease upon death? In some of the recently published letters of the Stracheys, these British analysts cattily discussed patients' problems, including, most notably, those afflicting one of James Strachey's most eminent patients, D. W. Winnicott. Is it ethical for biographers who gain access to such material to publish details about another individual who, although dead, arguably still has a right to the preservation of analytical confidentiality? Such conduct amounts to a kind of "outing" in which hidden aspects of the self are disclosed by someone who was never intended to know about them and is loyal only to an abstraction such as "history" or "biographical truth."

We shall use the practice of outing as an interesting parallel to a form of rage directed against anyone who would wish to keep his or her sexuality (or psychic life) private when disclosure of it would seem to be in someone else's more pressing interest. Advocates of mandatory reporting argue that the therapist must "out" his patient if the patient talks about a legislatively active topic. We may wonder if there is a particular envy of any person who has managed to find privacy in a self-disclosing society and who has further managed to say no to social and legal pressures to comply with forced disclosure. The person who says no demonstrates a capacity and an interior situation that is not so easily accommodated by individuals who feel no such right and who have managed this lack by identifying with the forces of adaptation. The homosexual man or woman who refuses to declare his or her sexual orientation in spite of pressure from gay rights advocates may simply be refusing a violation of privacy that should be guaranteed to all. Sexuality is one's own business unless for a particular political reason one decides to disclose it. What takes place in a clinical hour or in the course of a psychoanalysis is equally private, and disclosure should only occur if the patient permits it.

It is more difficult to reckon why, in light of the profound need for confidentiality if psychoanalysis is to work, organized psychoanalysis in the United States should have failed to organize any protest against the degradation of one of its essential conditions. To be sure, psychoanalysts have perhaps always viewed themselves as somehow removed from the fates suffered by other mental health professionals, and the idea that they would escape the interventions of the courts was a common one. Indeed, very few psychoanalysts have been compelled to hand over their clinical records. But this answer fails to address the question of why the legislative incursion on privilege would not alarm the analytic community into an organized protest against this part of their work in principle, even if all agreed that it was unlikely that they would be touched by the new laws—in principle, not only because it is wrong to have this invasion of clinical privacy, but also because, as we have argued in the previous chapter, abrogation of this right affects the atmosphere under which all analyses are conducted, whether immediately affecting any one analyst or not.

Action in the form of organized protest may not have occurred to psychoanalysts because theirs is hardly an activist profession. Indeed, the very virtues that sustain an analysis, as outlined in the previous chapter, especially the privileging of psychic life as opposed to actual life, favor any tendency by analysts toward a more removed and contemplative posture.

Further, analysts may feel that it is rather unseemly to express their alarm about social issues that affect the profession. Almost excessively concerned with how they will be regarded by relentlessly urbane and calm colleagues, few psychoanalysts have felt inclined to take up the chalice of confidentiality, even though they recognize its importance. ("Well, these things move in swings and roundabouts; it will go the other way. Let's not get all worried about it." "A mandatory disclosure of clinical notes is so unlikely that no one should get hysterical about it.") Political consciousness and political action within the domain of psychoanalysis seem to many analysts the preserve of the hysteric, overly saturated with identifications that pertain to the political province of the other and not the self, or worse, evidence of a paranoid disposition. To remain calm in stormy waters, whatever the cause, seems the best way for such analysts to remain psychoanalytic: assured, confident, and quiet.

The single deadliest blow to confidentiality by all mental health professionals, whether analyst or therapist, activist or quietist, is their collusion with managed care.[1] At first, analysts and therapists must have seen those insurance forms in which they were asked to declare a diagnosis and, once a quarter, to scribble a brief note on progress as an expression of the insurance company's legitimate right to know how matters were proceeding. Medical psychoanalysts, psychologists, and social workers, in any event, had long been accustomed to appropriate disclosures of details of treatment in the weekly case review sessions of the hospitals or clinics where they worked. Discussing a patient with an insurance company no doubt felt to many like a minor and legiti-

---

1. It is beyond the scope of our work to examine in detail parallel developments in other countries, but the devolution of the National Health System (the NHS) in the United Kingdom into trusts is part of a managerial "revolution" in which that corporate mentality that now generates the managed care systems in the United States is hard at work. The view of British psychoanalysts and psychotherapists that what is taking place in the United States "can't happen here" is belied by the erosion of analytical privilege that in many respects is greater than in the United States. Indeed, the regulatory abolition of the patient's right of confidentiality within the NHS is, if anything, more comprehensive than in an American HMO. The DHSS (Department of Health and Social Services) orders that clinical notes of a health professional are the property of the Health Authority and "ultimately of the Secretary of State." See Black et al. 1989, p. 27.

mate extension of such clinical discussions. But with the passage of time and the replacement of peer assessors working for the company, not by clinical experts but rather by cost-effectiveness clerks, analysts and therapists could no longer convince themselves that what they were passing on to the company was in confidence. No one knew and no one knows what the fate of such reports has been and will be.

It is exceedingly difficult to understand this development. While it is true that many beginning psychotherapists felt that for economic reasons they had no choice but to provide the reports, established therapists and analysts were customarily not in that position. Although some companies did pay for a substantial portion of analysis, most only paid for a limited number of annual sessions— something like 30.[2] Typically, then, the therapist would be paid by the patient for additional sessions in a given year. Often knowing that the company would pay only $80 an hour when the analyst charged $120, the patient would pay him the additional $40.

Why didn't the clinical professions, knowing that such accommodations were increasingly de-

_____

2. It is not difficult to sympathize with the dilemma insurance companies found themselves in with regard to coverage for mental disability. Determining how to provide coverage for a population in an economically feasible manner is still a challenging national problem.

structive of clinical work, organize meetings, discuss the matter, and launch effective protests?

Is it possible that a form of collusive corruption had long since been taking place, that is, that professionals had found a way to collude with the infringements of managed care and indeed to profit from them? If so, then this is hardly the atmosphere in which a professional feels inclined to raise issues about the ethics of the profession. Troubling as this conclusion might be, it is especially so for psychoanalysts. For while it might be argued that recently qualified psychologists, social workers, and others lack a tradition that values the preservation of privilege, the same cannot be said of psychoanalysts. Ethical and moral leadership should have come from within the analytical profession but did not, and the absence of any organized protest against the degradation of its essentials remains to this day a startling and disturbing fact.

Because psychoanalytical professional bodies are managed by part-timers who give volunteer hours to their organizations, they have not had the means adequately to assess or correct the progressive erosion of their profession. If psychoanalysts have been troubled by developments such as the overmedication of patients, the increasing evolution toward defensive practice, the labeling of patients, and the forensic fudging of important ethical boundaries, they have as professional organizations remained substantially silent. In part, this is due to splits among the professionals, but it may

also reflect a troubling uncertainty about the nature of psychoanalysis and its position in society.
Some psychoanalysts, for example, would defend
the simplistically stupefying effect of *DSM-IV* on
clinical practice.[3] They might point to its uses in
emergencies, where coming up with a diagnosis is
necessary to clinical actions in a hospital setting.
Indeed, if these primers were restricted to such
emergency conditions, put in their proper place as
temporary and simplistic devices for expedient reasons, they could be of use to all clinicians. But the
DSM-ing of America is an unfortunate extension of
the labeling of persons in a culture that seems
blindly resistant to individual idiom.[4] That such a

------

3. As a classification, *DSM-IV* is rather impressive. The clinical entities are as well presented as one could expect from
such an enterprise. Our critique is less with the book, per se,
than it is with the ultimate uses of this book and the failure
of the authors and the sponsoring professions to anticipate
misuse and to write the book with such social consciousness
in mind. Thus a cookbook like *DSM-IV* needs to incorporate
its own deconstruction, through greater attention to ambiguity in diagnostics, rather than avoid this issue by weakly
claiming that a person could easily fit several diagnoses at
one time. The authors of *DSM-IV* correctly anticipate the
effect of their publication by stating the criteria "are not
meant to be used in a cookbook fashion" (p. xxii), but if you
write a cookbook then . . .
4. In what reads as a remarkably disingenuous statement the
team that wrote *DSM-IV* states "A common misconception
is that a classification of mental disorders classifies people,
when actually what are being classified are disorders that

mass assignment of all selves into pigeonholes should take place in a country that every hand-on-the-heart day reminds itself of its freedoms is surprising only to those who are not psychoanalysts; this is a country that too often talks about freedom but enacts restriction.

DSM-IV demands that all clinicians fit their patients into categories that experienced analysts know to be spurious. Very few patients really exist within the simplistic confines of the labels in this book. Happily, people are more complex than that, and proper treatment is always more complex than clinical intervention aimed at a particular pathological type. But all too often there is both money and prestige in these labels. With every new diagnostic term comes yet another group who publish books, proclaim their expertise, and enjoy their profit.[5] In any city of the United States one can find experts on PDD, MPD, and now ADHD. The dull-

---

people have" (p. xxii). This is true in only the narrowest of readings and misleading, in our view, as the classification most definitely divides people according to personality types, e.g., borderline, narcissistic, etc.

5. Clearly there is an important distinction to be made between psychotherapists and psychoanalysts who write accounts of their work with patients who present unusual difficulties, such as the borderline or the eating disorder patient, and writers who aim to exploit the market by writing about any of the disorders in order to fill a recent publication space offered by a new edition of the *DSM* or the creation in the profession of a newly fashionable diagnosis, such as MPD.

ing effect of these acronyms reflects the intellectual retardation occasioned by such thinking.

Lest it be assumed that this simplistic categorizing of the individual is the effect only of eager beavers who wish to make a name for themselves, it bears mention that a surprising number of American works on psychoanalysis have an unmistakable "cookbook" organization. Whether it is the borderline, the narcissistic, or the eating disorder, some of these books tell fellow clinicians what such a person looks like, why they are the way they are, and what to do about it. The fact that no two patients in any of these categories is ever to be found in the same psychic boat is of no apparent consequence. Such books sell because there is now an

-----

It is not difficult to note a difference between a clinician who writes up what he has found to be true, and the more self-promoting publication, in which the clinician moves from his own, always limited experience of any patient or type of patient to the subtle claim of a categorical expertise, i.e., *the* way to treat the borderline or the eating disorder. Such "cookbooks" are not to be found in European or South American psychoanalytical writings, but one must hasten to add, that both the *DSM-IV* and American "cookbooks" do sell quite well in other countries. So if these formulas are not part of another culture's mentality, they nonetheless have their attractions. We believe it is important to see how a certain way of looking at and presenting psychoanalytical work with patients has been attractive to readers for all the wrong reasons and now comes home to roost in an aggressively prescriptive view of how to resolve mental conflict.

overwhelming need to have order forms for the treatment of classified souls. An unwitting side effect of what Kevin Hartigan (1994) calls "therapy by manual" is the production by managed care corporations of therapy manuals, which unfortunately come out of the cookbook approach to complex psychological processes. "In my mind," writes Hartigan, "therapy by manual bears as much resemblance to psychotherapy as paint-by-numbers does to art" (p. 5).

The creation of false expertise is an unfortunate result of the fact that psychoanalysis is not a science and could never propose that its findings were scientific. Even as that fact is no doubt frustrating to some psychoanalysts, who do often try to find some prior category for their discipline, considering it either as a science, a form of psychology, a kind of philosophy of the mind, a theology, or a poetics, its characteristics are too overdetermined to be so classified. It will take a long, long time indeed for psychoanalysis to come to anything like a convincing definition of itself.

Have therapists who need to escape the frustrating ambiguity of their professional status done so, in part, by creating false expertise? By assembling colleagues who agree with them and with whom perhaps, they can write books on a clinical topic, they can create the illusion that true science has taken place. But technical papers, conference appearances, and statistics about patients presumably suffering from a given syndrome or disorder are the trappings of expertise, not the substance. Lawyers in search of expert witnesses may use these trappings in court, but it is hardly surprising that many a juror regards these witnesses as mutually canceling.

Forensic "witnessing" to the mentally disturbed or the emotionally endangered suggests that after the fact analyses of the criminal personality establish a reliable science of prediction. Paul S. Appelbaum, M.D., draws attention to the implications of *Davis* v. *Lhim*. A patient voluntarily admitted to a hospital proceeded to kill his mother two months after discharge. She apparently tried to take his shotgun away from him and was killed in the effort. The patient had no violent history, although another hospital note two years prior to the murder indicated that he spoke threateningly about his mother. Citing *Tarasoff*, the Michigan court found the psychiatrists negligent. Appelbaum points out that *Davis* is a case that does not satisfy the *Tarasoff* criteria, as the patient was not dangerous at the time of admission, nor was he threatening an intended victim. Yet the court held that the psychiatrists should have "foreseen" the danger. "Many members of the public and the judiciary," writes Appelbaum, "genuinely believe that psychiatrists can predict when patients will be violent and, by implication, that they must be acting negligently if they fail to take steps to prevent violent acts." He concludes: "In part, the profession's overselling of its abilities during the past decades is coming home to roost" (American Psychiatric Association 1989, p. 43).

Indeed, as Derek Chiswick, an eminent forensic psychiatrist in Great Britain, tellingly points out, psychiatrists cannot predict dangerous behaviour on the basis of psycho diagnostics. Indeed, the only telling variable that permits anyone to reasonably assume that any individual might be dangerous are prior acts of violence! Referring to the practice of incarcerating in mental hospital individuals who pose a presumed dangerous threat to society, Chiswick sounds a note of caution: "This use of psychiatrists to legitimize, on the grounds of dangerousness, a punishment imposed for public protection should be deprecated—principally because *the prediction of dangerousness is not a matter on which psychiatry can speak with confidence*" (Chiswick 1995, p. 224, italics added).

The development of exaggerated or false expertise has led directly to the unconsidered development of collective fashions in the practice of psychotherapy. Without subjecting findings to intense critical review, psychotherapists have assumed expertise in how, for example, to resurrect repressed memories. Hundreds of clinicians—it is impossible to know just how many—jumped to false conclusions about patient reports and identified "perps," almost inevitably a parent, who then became vilified. Such false expertise and its destructive consequences have understandably damaged the reputation of all psychotherapies.

DSM-ing and the expert on one of its categories are of immediate interest not only to the legal profession, which believes it has found knowledge derived from clinical practice, but to the managed care industry as well. Indeed the authors of *DSM-IV* herald its forensic uses—"It may facilitate the legal decision maker's understanding of the relevant characteristics of mental disorders" (p. xxiv)—thus paving the way for lawyers and third-party providers to classify emotional conflicts in terms suited to their needs. In the last few years, the American Psychiatric Association has considered using the *DSM* as a standard with specified forms of treatment for the major classifications of illness. While psychoanalysts might cheer over the selection of psychotherapy as the preferred treatment for the obsessional personality disorder but lament the selection of medication for depression, they have failed to see the type of mentality that underwrites the entire enterprise.

The American Psychiatric Association has thus far produced three *Practice Guidelines*, each one constructed by a work group of six members, some 150 reviewer consultants, and solicited or submitted comments from some thirty-six organizations, including the American Psychoanalytic. The work group writes that "the guideline is written in successive drafts, each being revised on the basis of comments received from an increasing number of

people" and then the drafts go to the Steering Committee for review of the entire project. "Later drafts
are sent to members of the Assembly, the District
Branches, the Board of Trustees, and other APA
components." The final draft is sent to the Board
of Trustees for their approval and so "each guideline is reviewed by hundreds of psychiatrists and
other interested parties prior to publication." Indeed the list of references reads very much like the
assemblage of interested parties, a kind of "pork
bibliography" with a nod and a wink to these same
parties. This extraordinary political process, couched
in the language of science, trades on the myth that
if scientifically trained people, that is, psychiatrists,
pass the buck around, then this migration must be
a scientific act in itself. The APA thus creates the
illusion that thought-by-committee-passage is a
kind of human laboratory, as the text passes through
its many stages of examination.

The underlying disingenuousness of this project
becomes clear at several points. The back cover tells
us that the *Practice Guideline* takes its place among
"specific recommendations" rendered by psychiatry for over a hundred years, but under the "Statement of Intent" just inside, the booklet reads: "This
report is not intended to be construed or to serve
as a standard of medical care" (p. vii). In fact, at
the time of selection of personnel for the work
groups and the reviewers, the APA became aware
that the proposed guidelines were eagerly awaited
by two very important groups: the managed care

industry and the legal malpractice industry. They correctly anticipated that these guidelines would become the basis of officially sanctioned treatment, and thus open to immediate implementation by HMOs and the bottom line for malpractice suits.

Thus even though the "Statement of Intent" tries to convince the readers it is not what it is, adding that the psychiatrist must be the one who makes the final clinical judgment, the *Guidelines* are indeed standards of care. The *Practice Guideline for Major Depressive Disorder in Adults*, for example, proceeds to dictate a somatic intervention for depression.

> *Even in cases of mild depression*, if the symptoms do not respond to psychotherapy, somatic treatment should be considered. Optimal treatment of major depression that is chronic or is moderate to severe generally requires some form of somatic intervention, in the form of medication or electroconvulsive therapy, coupled with psychotherapeutic management or psychotherapy. [American Psychiatric Association 1993a, p. 10, italics added]

This advice all but nullifies psychoanalytic practice. What exactly is meant by "do not respond to psychotherapy?" To what effect? And over what period of time? Psychoanalysts, for example, know that many patients may endure mild to substantial depression brought about by the psychoanalytical process when they get more insightfully in touch with destructive sides of their personality, or when they delve into prior relations to a mother or a father that are deeply painful to recollect. In contemporary North America, however, what psychiatrist would feel that he could decline the recommendation of the *Practice Guideline*? As the guideline proceeds, the recommendation for medication is seconded in similar terms: "Even mild depression if unresponsive to nonsomatic treatment, should be considered for anti-depressant medication therapy" (p. 22). However understandable it is for psychoanalysts trained in psychiatry to want to participate in the political process described above, the honorable mention of psychoanalysis as one form of treatment in the booklet is obliterated by a series of predictable recommendations to medicate the depressed individual.

This marginalization of psychoanalysis by a national psychiatric association is not limited to the United States. Indeed, in Scotland, the Chief Medical Officer has issued two similar guidelines, one on anxiety, and the other on depression, which push psychotherapy completely out of the picture.[6] This has caused alarm among those consultant psychotherapists who now believe serious measures are being taken to remove psychotherapy from the health service in Scotland.

---

6. See "The Management of Anxiety and Insomnia," a report by the National Medical Advisory Committee. HMSO: Edinburgh, June 1994, and "Depressive Illness: A Critical Review of Current Practice and the Way Ahead," by the Clinical Resource and Audit Group. HMSO: Edinburgh, June 1993.

Practice guidelines turn out to be self-defeating. Managed care providers accept the recommended treatments and impose them as mandatory requirements, dictating to clinicians what they must do. If they do not do what the book says, then they are subject to action not only by the insurance company, but also by a patient or members of a patient's family who might in good faith believe that had another, "proper" procedure been followed, the patient would have been cured. Attorneys too eagerly embrace these simplistic prescriptions as if they constituted an authentic standard of care. Mass diagnoses and mass production of treatment are eradicating the discretely human—that is, the individual—scale of emotional disorders. Once an entire population can find a place in the new psychiatric cosmology, it can be serviced by the priests bearing the official cures, and all those who refuse this priesthood can be banished from the church.

These changes have occurred at an alarming rate. Coincidentally, there has been a considerable increase in the number of analytic practitioners. The 1980s saw the enfranchisement of hundreds of nonmedical psychotherapists, now grandfathered as psychoanalysts, and the birth of scores of psychoanalytic training centers across the United States. This increase in psychoanalytic practitioners corresponded with the wider application of the "duty to protect" to psychotherapists and psychoanalysts, and also with the *DSM*-ing of America. The codification of the new reporting requirements

in the ethical codes of individual psychoanalytic institutes and psychotherapy societies is beyond the
scope of our essay. Suffice it to say that in a further effort to establish their psychoanalytic credentials, many new societies devised ethical codes of
conduct that were far more severe than state requirements. It became ethical, in other words, to
become an advocate of the state, the managed care
provider, and the new Bible—the *DSM*.

By the 1990s any clinician working with a patient had a small colony of witnesses to include
consciously or unconsciously in the therapeutic
process. Notes were to be taken to chronicle one's
clinical judgments, addressed to attorneys and
managed care inspectors. The acting-out patient
who sexualized the transference brought up anxieties in the therapist about how this process might
appear to his professional society and/or to the state
licensing board. A southwestern state's licensing
board, for example, mandates that any therapist
who hears from a patient that any other therapist
has allegedly been behaving in an unprofessional
manner with a patient must immediately report
that therapist to the board. The board initiates an
investigation. Although it informs the therapist that
he is under investigation, it does not indicate the
charge or the source of the accusation. Repeated
efforts by clinical psychologists in the state to inform the board of the extremely destructive oppor-
tunities this system offers to an acting-out patient
have fallen on deaf ears.

An eminent psychologist (personal communication, l994) wrote a letter protesting actions in this particular state, pointing not only to the fact that complainees were left for as long as a year in suspense, not knowing the nature of the charge, but to the fact that any complaint must be reported to all third parties, which has the immediate effect of curtailing further referrals. Often the psychologists who are the investigators for the board are opposed to psychoanalytic psychotherapy; thus a behaviorist might be looking into a complaint against a psychoanalyst. The writer maintained that this arrangement had led to the use of threats to gain plea bargaining capitulation from the complainee. Indeed, the writer closed by bringing to the board's attention the fact that consumer groups were organizing workshops in how to file complaints to the board, encouraged to do so because complaints to a board did not involve the legal expenses incurred in a malpractice suit. Complaints entailed no fees for the patient but were financially draining for the accused psychologist.

Psychologists in this state may mislead themselves by believing that the Board of Examiners refuses to consider the destructive effects of this regulation because its members have always had a profound antipathy toward psychodynamic psychotherapy, but it is understandable why they might feel this way. The privilege that is meant to hold between a psychoanalyst and his patient is not a privilege that many psychologists and social

workers would support, not least because psychoanalysis and psychoanalytic psychotherapy are regarded as ill-founded. Members of Division 39, the
section on psychoanalysis of the American Psychological Association (APA), might wish to argue the
need for a revision of the APA ethics code so that
confidence can be breached under no circumstances, but such an effort would arouse only further antipathy. For the sad fact is that the APA
actually lobbied the state of California to be put
on the list of those professions mandated to report child abuse cases when they discovered that
psychologists had for whatever reason not been
included!

We have, in other words, reached a stage in the
practice of psychotherapy in which clinicians themselves oppose privilege on the grounds that the psychotherapist does indeed have a duty to protect. To
protect the child, to protect the woman who is being
stalked, to protect the potential victim of a crime,
to protect . . . well, who should not be protected?
Such practitioners argue that while one can and
does listen to the client's inner life, there are limits
to privilege that should be explained in the first
consultation (Kalichman 1993). As the laws, regulations, and ethical codifications mushroom, such
a clinician would, therefore, be informing a new-
comer that he is required by law to report any hint
of sexual abuse, physical abuse, or intended harm
against anyone else. Further, if the patient knows
of a friend in therapy who is distressed by alleged

malpractice of the therapist, this too will have to be reported. To the patient covered by managed care, the clinician would in honesty have to report that he will be sending in written reports to the provider on the progress of treatment and will from time to time be discussing the patient on the phone with a managed care provider. Further, he will ask the patient if he can now and then present him to a small clinical case conference or at a conference, when he will request the patient's permission to do so, and if requested, supply the patient with the name of the organization and the significant persons attending.

Each of these interventions may seem reasonable enough in itself to a lay person. And indeed, nothing is amiss if the aim of therapy is to promote social adaptation. As we will suggest in the next chapter, there is in all likelihood a need to separate the so-called helping professions, so that what we might think of as "social therapists" (see Chapter 5) could open practices that would indeed be the therapeutic embodiment of the state and its managed care. But if a psychoanalysis is to work, the psychoanalyst cannot inform his patient that he would have to be turned over to the authorities if certain facts were revealed. If this is how a pervert, for example, began his analysis, then the psychoanalyst would be nothing but an extension of the criminal justice system. He would be there to apprehend the patient.

Is it possible that the clinician-turned-cop reflects

an unconscious cultural attitude that what perverts
and their kin really need is apprehension and punishment rather than treatment? Is it possible that
the idea of a criminally inclined patient arouses a
certain rage in lawmakers and authorities who view
the psychoanalytic approach as a form of cosseting
the criminal? Is the attack on privilege an attack on
psychoanalysis itself?

Perhaps this is so. For it cannot have escaped
the court's comprehension, or that of managed care
providers, that these intrusions into psychoanalysis are destroying the profession. If the legal profession, for example, saw the lawyer–client privilege suspended by legislative decree in a sweeping
national mood of rage against the privileged life of
the lawyer, that profession would not be in any
doubt why this was happening and to what effect.
Now that psychoanalysts can feel the impact of
these intrusions into their practice, there is no
doubt in their minds that it has affected their ability to practice in general and most particularly with
certain key patients. An adolescent girl, for example, who hints in the first consultation that she
may have been abused may be referred to someone
else, as may a perverse patient who has pederastic
inclinations. A borderline-schizophrenic youth with
violent fantasies may be referred to a hospital to
protect the clinician. A paranoid woman in mid-life,
litigiously acting out her sense of injury, would be
referred, as would a man aggrieved at his wife's di-
vorce action, desperate to keep his children with

him, and certain that his wife has been a negligent and possibly abusive mother. The list is endless. Psychoanalysts, like obstetricians, are declining to treat patients not only because they fear the hassle such treatments might incur, but more to the point, because such patients evoke a mental context that makes the receptive function of psychoanalysis impossible. Psychoanalysis cannot function, not because the analyst would have to terminate treatment in the event of incursion into the clinical relationship, but because the clinical relationship cannot get off the ground to begin with.

It is a sad outcome that clinicians across the United States, in stark contrast to their European and South American colleagues, have begun to practice defensive psychotherapy. Patients are either given medication or referred to psychiatrists for medication, not because such treatment is actually warranted but because the clinician is anxious to be seen to have acted in such a way as to control the unfortunate effects of the patient's condition. The fact that in many respects such medications so dull the client's mentality that it is no longer possible to gain access to his or her internal life is not lost on the clinician, but he or she feels that this is a required sacrifice in the current climate. Where the clinician feels that there might be a mandatory report requirement or litigation deriving from the treatment, he will defend himself by zeroing in on these possibilities and focusing the treatment so that he can record in his notes a seemingly exhaustive effort to get to the source of the truth. This defensive stance has already produced considerable problems in its own right. Many clinicians, hearing a patient musing on a believed-in abuse, have felt duty-bound to help that patient objectify the abusing person, leading patient and therapist into a collusive witch hunt, to the creation of "false memories," and to yet another set of litigants demanding the release of clinical records—the aggrieved parent suing for damages.

Many clinicians, hearing from a patient who is wondering about the way his mother or father behaved toward him, inform the patient that if he continues to talk about the matter he is bordering on the mandatory reporting laws. He also warns the patient that they may unwittingly and in good faith create a false memory for which the therapist would be liable. (Consider, for example, the sad case of Paul Ingram, a deputy sheriff in Olympia, Washington who confessed to entirely fictitious acts of "satanic ritual child abuse" that he claimed to have remembered [Wright 1994].) Such liability, the therapist explains, is regrettable but a possibility and unfortunately he cannot work with the patient in this area because of that risk. This increased "legalization" of therapy, in which the therapist defends himself in the name of the legal implications, is another feature of defensive practice. The therapist sees himself in a potentially litigious situation and begins to defend himself, at cost to the patient, in the very early part of the treatment.

This outcome will seem almost unbelievable to many. And certainly in large cosmopolitan cities it is relatively rare. But in areas where the therapeutic community is, for different reasons, more vulnerable, such as the southwestern United States, this procedure is not uncommon. The degree of the problem is often known to those clinicians practicing in an area that suffers that atmosphere and to those analysts and clinicians who visit such an area. However, because of the still unorganized response of the mental health professions to these problems, there has yet to be sufficient sharing of this kind of knowledge, not to mention the studies needed to assess the degree and effect of defensive practice.

In what is surely a misguided act of reparation to the patient, for whom privacy has long since been removed by a therapist required to be an informant, the American Psychological Association deems in its ethics guidelines that all psychologists who wish to discuss a patient with a colleague must gain the patient's permission first. Given that this is the one situation where a clinician must be free to disclose, in confidence, what his patient says or does in order to gain supervision or to insure a private consultation, how ironic it is that this freedom too should be removed by a mandatory obligation! Many psychologists who try to follow this feature of the ethics code believe that it is the most intrusive of all. When a patient is asked if his clinician may present him to another psychoanalyst, what is he to make of the question? And what is he to do when told the name of the consulting analyst? These apparent "rights" almost perversely remove a freedom essential to the function of psychoanalysis that they presume to protect. Such a request for permission is needlessly disruptive and contributes to psychic disequilibrium in both patient and clinician. A sad outcome of this intrusion is the decrease in consultations, as therapists often come to the conclusion that it is not worth it to request one. That they should limit themselves in this way even with the paranoid patient, who often makes disturbing demands on the analyst, or with the dangerous (to self or other) patient for whom consultation is often important in the development of clinical judgment, is all the more dismaying.

The present trend in the destruction of privilege—and its ultimately devastating effect on the practice of psychoanalysis—is gloomy indeed. We have reflected on those elements that we believe have contributed to this erosion of an important human freedom, but we have only scratched the surface. As ours is an effort to bring this issue to immediate attention in order to stimulate appropriate action, we will now turn to the measures that could be taken to restore the profession.

5

RESTORING PRIVILEGE

The destruction of confidentiality by courts, state legislatures, managed care providers, biographers, and former therapists would seem to be so far advanced that attempts to reverse the process so as to restore the conditions essential to psychoanalysis may seem quixotic or worse.

If we begin with a premise that a patient who sees a psychoanalyst is guaranteed that absolute confidentiality is assured and maintained, then the door is shut to any and all requests from third parties for clinical notes and testimony by the clinician. Any psychoanalyst who listens to a patient describing the sexual molestation of a child would have to bear the considerable anguish of his position: spe-

cifically he would be obliged to refrain from trying
to protect the child by informing on the adult. He
may not disclose information that would reveal his
patient's identity because by doing so he destroys
the practice of psychoanalysis. His position is no
different than that of the journalist who must protect the source of an article, the lawyer who must
protect his client, the priest who must protect his
penitent. There can be no exceptions.

We propose that psychoanalytic societies and
organizations adopt the following clear statement
about confidentiality and privilege:

> The contents of a psychoanalysis are strictly con-
> fidential and any and all disclosures by the psycho-
> analyst—such as discussing a patient with col-
> leagues, arranging for a hospitalization, acting in
> the interests of a child patient—must be given in
> the understanding that confidentiality is main-
> tained and that in all circumstances privilege is
> retained by the psychoanalyst.

These principles leave psychoanalysts free to
seek consultations with colleagues, and to exercise
clinical judgment without breaching confidentiality, although they would have to ensure that
the patient's identity was concealed. But they
would prevent a psychoanalyst from reporting
material from a session under the current mandatory reporting laws or complying with most managed care requests for information, because such

compliance compromises the patient's right of confidentiality.[1]

What can a society do, however, to protect its
citizens (child and adult) from harm? What additional systems of care could be established to carry
out the "duty to protect"?

Virtually all developed nations have social care
systems and social workers or their equivalents who
operate them. Children who have been beaten by
their parents or those who suffer from sexual molestation usually, although not always, show the
signs of such harm. There is by now a vast literature on this subject, and teachers, youth club work-

---

1. It is of interest that the Committee on Confidentiality of
the American Psychiatric Association comes to an enlightened but rare view in their 1987 "Guidelines on Confidentiality." After reviewing the steps a psychiatrist should take to
prevent an unnecessary disclosure in a court, and bearing in
mind that "if the psychiatrist feels that disclosure would be
unethical or damaging to the patient, he or she should resist
within the full limits of the law," the "Guidelines" conclude
that if all appeals fail, "psychiatrists may, as a matter of conscience, still refuse to divulge the information requested,
although they then place themselves at risk of being held in
contempt by the court. When in doubt, ethical considerations
require that the psychiatrist give priority to the right of the
patient to confidentiality and to unimpaired treatment"
(p. 13). Unfortunately nothing like this view is even hinted
at in the Association's subsequent related documents: "The
Principle of Medical Ethics" (APA 1993) and "Opinion of the
Ethics Committee on the Principles of Medical Ethics" (APA
1993).

ers, coaches, and the lay public are increasingly
aware of these signs. The dissemination of information about abuse will no doubt continue, so that
when a child is seen to be endangered, social services are notified and a social worker makes an
assessment. Although this procedure is open to
error—the more spectacular mistakes are the ones
reported in the media—social workers save thousands of children each year from abuse.

The uncertainty and confusion within the mental health professions around the question of confidentiality may be substantially resolved if the specific tasks of each discipline are more clearly
outlined. Many people will seek training in psychiatry, psychology, and social work because they wish
to help their clients in any way possible—by talking,
to be sure, but also by engaging identified "harm-
ers" (parents, spouses, partners) in the patient's treatment, by actively soliciting other agencies and individuals to intervene in the patient's life (child welfare
officers, lawyers, the police), and by willingly offer-
ing a paralegal service, that is, by testifying in court
or related proceedings. We might refer to such a
practitioner as a social therapist, not to be confused
with a social worker. Although it is logical in some
respects for social workers to become social therapists—and many would—it is also the case that social workers have been committed to psychoanalysis and psychoanalytic psychotherapy since the
1920s. Indeed the category of social therapist would
allow many social workers to opt clearly for psychoanalysis, which is difficult to do given the fact that

the title that defines them suggests a type of work that they often do not do. Among the clients seeking help from social therapists would be any victim of an injury suffering from traumatic effect and needing to talk about it. We may assume that the initial aim of treatment might be to provide the support and strength needed to deal with the trauma. A different sort of patient might need to cool down. A social therapist could offer such a person a way to approach the authorities in order to find the safety of preemptive custody.

The client–social therapist relation would be an advocacy partnership. The therapist would not only discuss the client's feelings but would also explore, initiate, support, and carry out practical actions that would help resolve the problem. At all times it would be understood that any criminal act the client discussed would be reported, as required by law. However, prospective clients, like arrested suspects, would have to be read their rights *before* entering this partnership. Such therapists would therefore want to post in their waiting rooms a notice spelling out the terms of the relations. Psychologists, whose ethical guidelines ordain that they inform the patient of the limits of confidentiality, among other matters, at the very beginning of treatment,[2] already provide such notice.

---

2. Principle 5 of the Code of Conduct of the American Psychological Association decrees that "where appropriate, psychologists inform their clients of the legal limits of confidentiality" (Casebook, 67).

A child who seemed to a teacher to be in some difficulty—depressed, often coming to school with bruises, with parents known to be violent—might be referred to a social therapist who would work with the child and also intervene in the child's actual circumstances. A pervert who confessed to a social therapist that he was photographing young children would talk through with the therapist how his actions must be reported and how to do so most constructively. The therapist would continue to work with the client through his arrest, visit him in detention, provide further support during the trial, remain in some meaningful contact for the duration of a prison sentence, and, upon release, assist the client to rebuild his life.

Social therapists already exist within at least three important disciplines: social welfare, social psychiatry, and social psychology. By definition, social workers were originally employed by social agencies to work with individuals and families in distress. Educators, general practitioners, social welfare agencies, voluntary services (e.g., women's shelters) and others will often want to refer to an individual—either a potential victim or perpetrator of harm—to a social therapist for assessment and assistance. Such persons and agencies should be informed of progress and outcome. We view such assistance as essential to all societies and the expression of an important and legitimate tradition of social policy and social work.

However, people also need another kind of help.

There must be another kind of therapist—broadly put, the private psychotherapist[3]—who is not a social therapist and who does not function as a mediator between the state and the client. All persons seeing a psychoanalyst, for example, must do so in absolute confidence, no matter what they have done, contemplate doing, or have suffered from someone else. This arrangement, too, would have to be exceptionally clear, and although it might seem indecorous in the waiting room, it would be essential to have this principle posted for prospective patients, a kind of reverse Miranda; they should read what is *not* going to happen as a result of their disclosures.

Those seeking to become therapists or psychotherapists should be able to choose what kind of practitioners they wish to become. Social therapists and private psychotherapists would still hail from their own varied schools of thought and the two generic classes would be clearly distinguished by the issue of confidentiality. "Confidentiality is guaranteed" is clear enough. Many present practitioners who are interested in psychoanalytic theory and psychotherapy would not accept this condition, and they might well opt to become affiliated with so-

---

3. From this point on we shall use the word *therapist* to refer to workers who offer a nonpsychoanalytic orientation, for example, social therapists, massage therapists, and cognitive therapists, reserving the word *psychotherapist* for practitioners working psychoanalytically.

cial therapy. That they might do so under the spe-
cies "psychoanalyst-social therapist" is fair enough,
insofar as they have the perfect right to create their
own hybrid. As long as the therapist's Miranda is
posted—that they do not guarantee confidentiality—the public will be properly informed.

Many social workers, for example, would choose
to be identified as private psychotherapists, and
rightly so. In turn, there are undoubtedly some clinicians who are psychoanalysts but would opt for
practice as a social therapist, or a hybrid of the two.
The obligation one has is ultimately to make it clear
to the prospective patient the fundamental terms
of the clinical relation: Is it strictly confidential, or
is privilege qualified?

As we have written we are in agreement that any
society has a right to protect itself from dangerous
individuals—those who would intend child abuse
or those who would plot violent acts. Social workers and psychiatrists have always been on the front
line of such social concerns, and the special bur-
dens assumed by these professions in their work
warrants not only recognition in our discussion,
but also distinction that would enable us to more
clearly see how the roles of the psychiatrist and the
work of the psychoanalyst diverge.

Psychiatrists around the world have always had
to live in two worlds: the private sphere of work
with the disturbed patient and the public domain
of their responsibility to protect individuals against
harm. The Royal College of Psychiatry in its "Posi-

tion Statement on Confidentiality"[4] indicates just how delicate a path the psychiatrist must tread in the modern world. On the one hand, it notes that psychiatrists must be especially alert to unwitting infringements on the patient's privacy; there is in general, the report states, "a much more widespread sharing of general information" (p. 3), partly facilitated by ordinary technology such as the photocopy machine, which makes dissemination of documents much easier than before, and partly occasioned by changes in social policy, in which, for example, a patient may consent to a request for information from a housing authority that has asked to contact the patient's medical practitioner. The psychiatrist must be alert to any unnecessary disclosures of information.

However, in the section marked "Special Situations in Adult Forensic Psychiatry," the Royal College firmly states (unwittingly echoing the *Tarasoff* opinion) that confidentiality ends "where the public interest duty to the community may override the confidence duty" (12). It concludes that "the courts may require information from case notes to be disclosed," thereby emphasizing the clinician's duty to keep adequate notes and to be mindful of his forensic obligations.

Nigel L. G. Eastman (1987), a prominent forensic psychiatrist in England who is also a barrister, finds a solution for problems that arise from the

---

4. Available from the Royal College of Psychiatry.

clinician's divided loyalties in what he sees as the contractual (as opposed to the tort) basis for confidentiality. He describes the basic contract as follows: "The patient, when deciding to disclose information, balances the harm (and the risk thereof) resultant from any breach of confidentiality against the benefit which he perceives as flowing from the clinician's services" (p. 53). Eastman defends his theory as libertarian (as opposed to paternalistic): "The notion of a confidentiality contract, freely and knowingly negotiated, maximizes the client's freedom of choice. So far as possible, it also equalizes the strength of the client and the clinician" (p. 57).

The scope of this book does not permit a thorough analysis of Eastman's argument, but one point is important. The patient's or client's freedom of choice and freedom to negotiate are real and meaningful only if we forget about the unconscious. As legal reasoning, Eastman's "libertarian" perspective is appealing, but like the *Lifschutz* opinion in California, which shares some of its underlying assumptions about freedom of choice (applying them to the notion of waiver), it ignores Anne Hayman's "essential point" that the client or patient is not—cannot—be aware of unconscious motives that may affect his contract "negotiation." At best, such motives make any true "meeting of the minds," the essential condition of contract formation, difficult to achieve; at worst, they make it illusory.

It may be that this problem makes a tort theory of confidentiality more satisfactory. Such a theory, which emphasizes the clinician's duty toward his patient and the consequences of breaching that duty, may be more paternalistic than Eastman's contractual framework. However, it has the advantage of greater realism about the actual strengths and weaknesses of the parties involved.

In any event, we would take issue with Eastman's conclusion that "[t]here can never be total agreement within a profession as to the solution of any particular such [confidentiality] problem" (p. 57). In fact, clergymen, journalists, and, as Eastman himself notes, lawyers ("There is an absolute right of confidentiality, in law, between the client and his lawyer") (56)—all seem to have reached something like "total agreement" about the basic principles of confidentiality in their professions. Why should psychoanalysts not be able to do the same by recognizing—and defending—the bedrock importance to their work of an "absolute right of confidentiality"?

There will always be a need for clinicians who are working under the kinds of divided obligation that Eastman analyzes: divided, that is, between the patient's private conflicts and some public good. However, precisely because psychiatrists have, by training, statutory obligation, and professional code, undertaken this role as a social therapist, it is critical to pinpoint the differences between what the psychiatrist can do and can offer and what the psychoanalyst can do and can offer.

The fact that the parent disciplines—psychiatry,

psychology, and social work—are irrevocably divided over these issues is not surprising as there are fundamental and irreconcilable differences between those who see themselves as private psychotherapists and those who work in the social psychological field. For a very long time now many psychoanalysts have urged their colleagues to declare their independence from other disciplines. Nothing would seem to bring the need for this independence more urgently into focus than the question of confidentiality. For that very precise creation that is psychoanalysis cannot be guaranteed by psychiatrists, psychologists, or social workers, who after all represent disciplines with vast and complex agendas. Indeed, as we have suggested, these professions are in many respects hostile to psychoanalysis.

One of the deterrents to organized political protection of psychoanalysis by its own practitioners is the divisions within the profession. There are several national organizations of psychoanalysis that have, at best, rather strained relations with one another. Always there are the inevitable questions: Who has the right to call him- or herself a psychoanalyst? Who is in possession of the one true path? While it is undeniable that some institutions offer superior training, not unlike colleges or universities, it is time for all psychoanalysts, it seems to us, to agree that anyone who has qualified in a psychoanalytic or psychoanalytic psychotherapy training program may practice psychoanalysis. Including

the psychoanalytic psychotherapist will undoubtedly raise hackles, and we do not wish to enter the
debate over the differences between psychotherapy
and psychoanalysis. As a movement, psychoanalysis is best served by generosity of spirit. We are of
the view, moreover, that whatever differences prevail between the practice of psychoanalytic psychotherapy and psychoanalysis, they are minor compared to their shared differences from all other
forms of treatment. Psychoanalysts will always be
able to identify themselves in other ways. A Lacanian psychoanalyst can indicate his affiliation with
a Lacanian society, and so too for an ego psychologist or a Kohutian.

Psychoanalysis will have to become an independent discipline and profession that generates its
own standard of ethics. And among the very first
canons of the ethical code would be a clear statement of the unqualified confidentiality of the patient—
psychoanalyst relationship. But the conflict of
interest that is intrinsic to the life of those psychoanalysts who still maintain a serious loyalty, consciously or not, to the discipline of origin, whether
psychiatry, psychology, or social work, may under-
mine even the effort of the International Psychoanalytical Association (IPA) to state clearly the right
of confidentiality. The recent "Draft Code of Ethical and Professional Conduct" approved at the IPA
Executive in July 1991 suggests in the section on
confidentiality that "a psychoanalyst may not reveal
the confidence entrusted to him in the course of his

professional work . . . except as required by law."
This exception sanctions and indeed codifies reporting. The section proceeds to outline what the
psychoanalyst should do if "required by law" to give
testimony, unaware apparently that agreement to
testify even where one would prefer not to do so,
amounts to an abandonment of the right of confidentiality. Although this is only a draft proposal and
even if adopted only a broad guideline—each member society will retain its own specific code of ethics—this IPA draft reveals what we take to be a
particularly North American agenda by creating
innumerable exceptions to privilege; it seems designed to accommodate the current statutory, regulatory, and third-party incursions on confidentiality in the United States.

The good news is that, as befits its political responsibility to provide leadership to the profession,
the IPA is giving serious thought to codifying psychoanalytical ethics. Other sections of this document, especially the guidelines on procedure for the
investigation and judgment of psychoanalysts engaged in unprofessional or unethical behavior, will
significantly improve the current situation. The
draft code is just that—a draft—and the IPA has requested all psychoanalytical societies and institutes
to discuss it and to recommend changes, thus ini-
tiating a comprehensive review of ethical issues
among its members, which is no small accomplishment in itself.

To be sure, adoption of a code such as we have recommended would place psychoanalysts in conflict with state reporting laws, certain regulatory requirements, parent-discipline codes of conduct, and third-party demands. Legal disputes would follow as psychoanalysts refused to provide the mandated disclosures. As uncomfortable as this situation would be, we are convinced that this strategy is the right thing to do. It would also create a substantial benefit. While in the past individual psychoanalysts who resisted handing over their clinical notes faced legal action without the support of their profession or their colleagues, psychoanalysts can in the future point to a clear code of ethics backed up by a national professional association, perhaps a confederation of those groups that would practice under the name of psychoanalysis. The only confederation with muscle that exists at present is the National Coalition of Mental Health Professionals and Consumers, Inc. (Box 438, Commack, New York), which is a grass-roots organization of mental health professionals, consumers, and consumer advocates. It illustrates how a national organization can bring people from very different backgrounds and points of view together into a common cause in a relatively short period of time. In our view, the psychoanalytic organizations would do well to follow the model of the coalition in bringing people together for effective representation. Another organization, the Consortium for Psychotherapy, which originated in Boston as a multidisciplinary lobby advocating change in national policy on managed care, also demonstrates how psychotherapists can organize effectively.

Psychoanalysts have already begun to consider legal remedies for deceptive or fraudulent practices by some managed care organizations. It may be that the federal Employee Retirement Income Security Act (ERISA) provides a remedy for employees whose plan promises benefits that are effectively denied through the use of vague criteria, e.g., a refusal to authorize treatment for depression because it is not a "serious" disorder (see Stephens 1994). The position we advocate is based not on contractual rights but on the equally fundamental rights to privacy and to treatment itself. Litigation is an unpleasant prospect. However, we submit that it is better for the profession to take to the courts to defend its integrity and its very existence than to become an unwitting and helpless participant in its own destruction.

One cannot read the future, of course. However, it is at least reasonable to suggest that courts that continue to emphasize that confidentiality is essential to psychotherapy and that psychotherapy itself brings recognizable social benefits are unlikely to impose stiff penalties on psychoanalysts who refuse to turn over case notes for counsel. Indeed, California cases, at least, indicate that a principled stand by psychoanalysts on this issue would meet with judicial approval and perhaps even protection. For some time it may be that clinicians will suffer the fate of journalists who irritate the magistrate by sticking to principles. Such adherence might result in a custodial sentence, but if so, for only a very short time: a few days, as in the Lifschutz case, at the very most a few weeks. In time, however, as psychoanalysts make it clearer to the judiciary and to the public that their ethic demands preservation of confidence under all circumstances, their stand will meet with the same approval granted to other, similarly principled groups.[5]

---

5. There is an interesting parallel in the recent case of Oscar B. Goodman, a Las Vegas attorney whose client was suspected by federal prosecutors of involvement in organized crime. The attorney refused to comply with a court order to disclose records of payments to him by his client, claiming that the government subpoena would force him to testify against his client in violation of his ethical duty. The attorney paid contempt fines that eventually came to $50,000. He turned over the records only when his client gave him permission to do so and when the government threatened to bring criminal contempt proceedings that could result in disbarment. A thousand members of the National Association of Criminal Defense Lawyers wrote to the Justice Department to protest its treatment of Goodman. That organization and others have also supported Gerald B. Lefcourt, a lawyer who sued the Internal Revenue Service over a requirement that lawyers name clients who pay fees in cash of more than $10,000 in a given year. (See Richard Bernstein, "Lawyer Risks Jail to Protect Client Information," *The New York Times*, December 23, 1994, p. A14.)

State regulatory requirements would also require legal representation for clinicians who refuse
to comply. Some practitioners might lose state licenses to practice—as psychologists, psychiatrists,
or social workers. Again, however, assistance from
a national confederation of psychoanalytic organizations could help defray legal expenses and, just
as important, provide support for psychoanalysts
who resist. Psychoanalytic organizations could pe-
tition such agencies on behalf of a colleague who
was not in compliance with regulations for ethical
reasons. In the final analysis, however, psychoanalysis will have to become a separate profession
bearing its own name and licensed by the state
regulatory agencies.

This discussion may seem melodramatic to psychoanalysts who wonder how they could possibly
resist laws they know to be incorrect. We wish to
indicate a clear direction that the profession could
take to ensure that its practitioners are supported
and not left to fend for themselves. Perhaps the
knowledge of such support could in turn promote
conscientious action by individual psychoanalysts.

It is less easy to imagine the outcome of a clash
of codes of ethics between, say, the American Psychological Association and a new national confederation or coalition of psychoanalysts. Psychologists who belong to both would find themselves
caught between the APA's dictum that psychologists
must disclose and the national coalition's edict that
exceptions to confidentiality are impermissible

under any circumstances. Perhaps the APA will qualify its ethical code to accommodate such a position, in recognition of its integrity, even if many in the APA would disagree.

The remedy for the erosion of confidence created by cooperation with managed care seems to us more obvious. Since at the present time this information is not disclosed in confidence—not, that is, as a clinician to a clinic director or in consults with a colleague—psychoanalysts should refuse under any circumstances to cooperate with managed care institutions. There may come a time, perhaps under a national health care system, when psycho-analysts or psychoanalytically trained professionals could receive such reports and determine in their view whether coverage should be supplied and for how long, but we are a long way from any such state of affairs. Indeed, agreement of psychoanalysts to collude in what they well know to be a serious degradation of the ethics of their profession has done enormous damage to the practice of psycho-analysis.

No doubt the refusal to cooperate will mean that managed care providers will turn to other profes-sionals for referral. So be it. Already, the compro-mises required by such providers of psychotherapy has made a grotesque joke of such "provision." In-creasingly providers are turning to medication and limiting the number of talking sessions as they put what they regard as cost-effectiveness ahead of the needs of patients. It is hard to imagine in what way

a psychoanalyst's cooperation with such degradation helps any of his patients.

On the other hand, psychoanalytic societies and
organizations will have to give increased attention
to how to make psychoanalysis or psychoanalytic
psychotherapy available to people who cannot ordinarily afford it. Annual conferences of psychoanalytic clinics would go a long way toward form-
ing an association of clinics that could establish not
only a referral system, from city to city or region
to region, but also pool information on how to best
provide reduced-fee care.

Psychoanalysts will also have to devise an alternative way to manage the abusive patient, a solution that does not involve abrogation of confidentiality. In the United Kingdom, even though child
abuse is against the law, clinicians can still operate in a productive gray area. One clinician saw a
husband and wife in consultation, and it transpired
that the husband had been sexually molesting his
two preadolescent daughters for several years. He
had fondled their genitals and stroked their but-
tocks. His wife found out and gave him an ultima-
tum: either he sought treatment or she would leave
him and take the children with her. He was in other
respects quite a decent man—hard working, loyal,
supportive. But he was childlike and impulsive, and
on certain occasions when he was depressed would
crawl into one of the daughters' beds and be overcome with excitement. The entire family was referred to a clinic where the father received indi-

vidual treatment, the wife counseling, and the children psychotherapy. The problem was successfully worked through and the family remained intact. The father's problem, which had been deeply disturbing and confusing to his children and also to his wife, became an object of the whole family's right to redress. Only in this case the father was also included—included because as is so often the case with perverts, the perverse individual is *also* very troubled by his compulsions, and is in important respects victimized by his own mental illness.

We hope that in the course of time an intermediate solution can be found for the management of the abusive individual, something between no action at all and criminal prosecution. Although we maintain that there can be no incursions on patient–psychoanalyst confidentiality, this principle does not preclude the psychoanalyst from encouraging his patient to agree to the collaborative assistance of other mental health professionals, assistance that does not result in a prison sentence but in therapeutic intervention. A patient, then, who informed his psychoanalyst that he was molesting a child in the family could be assured that the child would be referred to a clinician for treatment and the wife for counseling, and the clinic would function as a responsible partner for the remediation of the problem.

Indeed, psychoanalysts will recognize such an arrangement as the reflection of nothing more nor less than clinical judgment, courses of action decided upon by the psychoanalyst in the interests of the patient. Very few of the situations now envisioned by mandatory reporting laws are beyond the purview of the psychoanalyst's clinical judgment. Ironically enough, were he free to undertake actions of his own choosing, he actually has at his disposal more effective extraclinical remedies than those currently ordained under the reporting laws. It is more effective to get an abusing parent into treatment and to have the other members of the family seen immediately by fellow practitioners than to call in the police. A patient who is intending to harm another person is not by any means beyond his psychoanalyst's remedial action. A psychoanalyst can, if in his view it is warranted, have a patient committed or sectioned in the hospital if the person is a threat to himself or others. To be sure, a patient may feel that he has been betrayed and some might break off further treatment, but the psychoanalyst does not disclose what the patient has said to him nor does his action result in a dire consequence to the patient. By exercising his judgment he can act with a greater range of options than he can under the current reporting laws, which mandate reporting to the police and lead only to incarceration.

If the patient is harming someone outside the family, such as a neighbor child, or stalking a woman with intent to rape her, the matter becomes more complex; it would be exceedingly difficult to intervene without bringing the patient to imminent prosecution and without violating privilege. One would have to imagine a cultural transformation, from the present climate of sanctimonious rectitude to a more thoughtful society that understands that sexual crimes are psychological compulsions that deeply disturb the perpetrator and for which there should be a therapeutic option. Were there changes in the American mentality, one could imagine encouraging a patient to inform social services of the identity of a child at risk or the woman being stalked. Such a disclosure would result in assistance for the individuals at risk. In other words, if the psychoanalyst were free to exercise his clinical judgment, he could both protect his patient and the potential victims.

And what of the murderer? Would a man intending to kill someone conceivably cooperate with the authorities, to the point of warning an intended victim? Because of the extreme sensitivity of this subject matter it is hard to gather sufficient evidence to know. But potential murderers do seek treatment. The authors know a psychoanalyst in a South American country who has had in analysis for many years a man who stalked women. The patient had exceedingly violent fantasies of murdering these women, but at the time of seeking help, exercised this compulsion by buying animals, taking them to his house, killing them, and covering himself in their urine and feces. There is no question in the psychoanalyst's mind, or in the minds of those with whom he has discussed the case over the years, that his patient would have proceeded to kill one of the women he stalked had he not been in treatment. But intense analytical work, five times a week, meant that over time the inner scenarios this patient was on the verge of acting out were expressed and analyzed in the sessions, and his stalking stopped, as did his killing of animals.

No doubt, many criminals are beyond therapeutic help. We do not propose a misplaced therapeutic optimism as the solution to violent crime. We do believe, however, that a violent virtue in the mentality of a society does more harm than good and prevents those individuals who could take and use treatment from doing so. We also think that some potential murderers who gained treatment do not go on to murder because of that treatment. At the same time, we remain skeptical about the efficacy of warning potential victims or of informing the police, who in similar situations—recurrent spousal abuse, for example—often confess themselves unable or unwilling to act before an actual crime has been committed. We submit that if there were a principle of limited indemnity, a patient who was abusing a child or harming others could identify the victim and in turn identify himself, if he was at least in the very first instance protected from a prison sentence. The psychoanalyst's clinical judgment, finally, is a more effective means of managing the criminally deviant patient than the mandatory reporting laws.

What about the patient who is a victim of an unethical action by a psychoanalyst, specifically, those analysands who have been sexually molested by the clinician? Is it not possible that a clinician could use privilege as a means of refusing to discuss a patient's claim that he acted in an improper manner? He would have to do so, in our view, if he were approached by the courts or by attorneys. We must reiterate that there are no circumstances in which the psychoanalyst can disclose what has been taking place with his patient that would not violate confidentiality. But he is liable to ethical investigation by his colleagues. All psychoanalytic societies have codes of ethics and ethical committees and over the years, when a psychoanalyst is found to have sexually molested a patient, the societies usually take action.[6] The *Journal of the American Psychoanalytic Association*, for example, prints the name of an offending psychoanalyst, at the same time indicating that such a psychoanalyst has been removed as a member of the association.

---

6. There are troubling situations in which psychoanalytical societies do not bring action against members who have committed unethical actions, and the IPA draft document addresses this problem. But as long as psychoanalysis does not see itself as a profession, issues of malpractice have too often been viewed as matters for the parenting profession, so psychoanalytical societies wait for medical associations or psychological associations to take action against the colleague.

Indeed, precisely because privilege is so essential to the function of psychoanalysis, when that privilege is abused by a psychoanalyst, such as in the fortunately infrequent cases of sexual molestation or other forms of abuse, it is essential for the analytic community to act vigorously and decisively. Patients must be assured that if they have the profound misfortune to be with a disturbed psychoanalyst, there is a readily available means of seeking consultation within the profession of psychoanalysis.

If psychoanalysts are to recapture the responsibility for self-regulation—one increasingly taken away by laws that criminalize abusive actions by psychoanalysts and psychotherapists—then the profession must consider how to inform prospective patients of their rights. It is not surprising that a patient turns to a lawyer when troubled by a psychoanalyst's actions. As we have argued, psychoanalysts should have posted in clear view in their waiting rooms an ethics code and a telephone number for any patient to call should he or she wish to lodge a complaint. At the end of an assessment consultation a clinician could hand to a prospective patient a brochure containing the code as well as appropriate addresses and telephone numbers, telling the patient that all psychoanalysts are required to do so. Information should be provided about exactly what the process entails. In this way, patients would learn what to do if the psychoanalyst behaved unprofessionally. Psychoanalytical societies already have ethics committees but we cannot assume that a patient knows the name of the psychoanalyst's society or—a much more intimidating matter—how to approach it. Psychoanalytical societies are hardly known for their receptivity to drop-in callers, phone or otherwise.

A posted ethics code in the waiting room and a distributed brochure, plus standard and clear procedures by a national confederation of psychoanalytical societies, would go a long way toward changing the understandable view by legislatures, state regulatory agencies, and the public that psychoanalysts do not regulate themselves well. A lawyer who is disbarred is known to have been effectively punished by his association. If he then suffers criminal prosecution, as well he may, as may a psychoanalyst who abuses a patient, at least the profession has preserved its integrity by taking the first step.

We believe, then, that a psychoanalyst who has abused a patient, while taking refuge in privilege in the courts, could not do so with a group of colleagues. His removal from practice by his professional association would then be an effective and appropriate punishment.

Internal tribunals could also provide the appropriate forum to which one psychoanalyst could effectively report suspected unprofessional conduct of a colleague. A recent incident reveals the need for such a forum. A psychoanalyst received distressed telephone calls from a patient of another psychoanalyst in a different city. Eventually the patient informed him (for the sake of clarity we will call him the consultant) that she was sleeping with her psychoanalyst. It was clear to the consultant that the patient was deeply regressed and potentially suicidal. It was also his clinical judgment that whether or not she had in fact been sleeping with her psychoanalyst, she needed to feel that the consultant believed her absolutely; this belief would allow her to get the help she needed from an independent consultation in her own city. The consultant therefore wrote a strongly worded fax supporting her account of the event. To have used a phrase like "alleged actions of your psychoanalyst" in his view would have been read by the distressed patient as a subtle indicator of disbelief.

Even though his actions resulted in her gaining an immediate independent consultation, it was deeply unfortunate that his letter to her was subsequently used by the patient's attorney in a claim against the psychoanalyst in question. The attorney did so over the objection of the consultant, who rightly pointed out that he had been in no position to determine the validity of the patient's claims and that his letter was a response to her emotional needs, not an assessment of the truth. Given the nature of analytical confidentiality, the consultant could not contact the defendant's attorneys and it troubled him that quite possibly his limited clinical work with the patient had been exploited by a legal team to potential abuse of the psychoanalyst in question. If psychoanalytical societies, in accordance with national guidelines, had stipulated that any psychoanalyst accused of unprofessional conduct or any psychoanalyst privy to such an allegation should so inform the ethics committee, then a tribunal created by that committee could hear clinical evidence from both sides and come to a judgment, thus avoiding the unfortunate situation described above.

Psychoanalysts who commit, for example, a sexual transgression should be held accountable by their profession. If found guilty of this violation of their professional obligations, they could be required to suspend practice for one or two years and at the same time be required to reenter analysis. We believe they should return all fees to the abused person. Were there subsequently to be a further sexual enactment, we think the psychoanalyst in question should permanently lose his right to practice. If the psychoanalytic profession can establish its own tribunals, then the fortunately rare patients who have suffered an abusive act from the psychoanalyst will be well served.

In return, however, if a clinician is falsely accused or if an ethics inquiry cannot come to a firm decision, then the arrangement we propose would protect the accused, who could not respond in another forum because of the strictures on disclosure. For example, the psychoanalyst who worked with Jeffrey Masson, whom Masson accused in considerable detail of gross negligence, was presumably prevented by privilege from defending himself.

Unsubstantiated allegations against psychoanalysts can be extremely damaging and in the type of situation described above, the psychoanalyst and his association should call for an internal inquiry. There the former patient should be free to make his case and the psychoanalyst to do the same. Although a jury of psychoanalysts might find it as difficult to know whom to believe, as might any other jury, it is our view that such an arrangement is better than nothing at all and also better than relying on lawsuits for civil damages.

The psychoanalytical profession at international and national levels must also deliberate over the proper fate of clinical records and the writing of psychoanalysis. It is our view that confidentiality is timeless. No person seeking an analysis should *ever* have his or her identity published without permission. As one cannot gain permission from the dead, no deceased patient can agree to such a request. Usually this problem arises, however, with the clinical records of deceased psychoanalysts. What is to be done with them? Often such records are left with a spouse who does not know how to dispose of them. In good conscience, some give them to institutions, such as a university, without giving careful thought to the possible violations of confidentiality that may result from such an act. One psychoanalyst looked up the papers of an eminent deceased colleague, held in another country, only to find that the library was open and that the clinical records of well-known patients were

there for anyone to read. This possibility was entirely due to lapse of consciousness by the institu-
tion in question. As these records had only been
deposited recently, fortunately their existence in the
library was not known and there were no violations
of confidence.

Psychoanalysts who wish for whatever reason
to leave their clinical records for posterity should
so indicate in writing and gain written permission
from their patients. Further, it is our view that each
local society should bear the responsibility of stor-
ing any deceased psychoanalyst's records. A psychoanalyst as he or she nears retirement should indicate to the society whether the clinical records are
to be preserved. It is easy to imagine that with a particularly gifted psychoanalyst, one whose work
would be of potential teaching value, such records
are well worth preserving. A psychoanalyst working with highly unusual and difficult patients, such
as murderers, perverts, or psychopathic children,
may want his records preserved for the general pool
of knowledge. Psychoanalytic societies, knowing
who these people are likely to be, would want at a
certain point, for example when such a clinician
reaches 60 years of age, to write to the psychoanalyst indicating that their clinical records are of
scholarly or professional interest. At this point,
patients could be contacted, permissions obtained,
and those who have so agreed would be informed
that upon the psychoanalyst's death the records
would be housed at the local society. It would be

important, as well, to spell out when the records would be available (e.g., in 50 years' time) and to whom they would be available (e.g., only to another psychoanalyst, or also to a biographer, or to the general public).

In the same spirit, psychoanalysis must determine clear guidelines for the publication of clinical material. We agree that losing the ability to write up clinical cases would be a mortal blow to the intellectual development of psychoanalysis. If, as we argue, confidence must be maintained under all circumstances, how can writing about a patient ever be warranted?

Publication is ordinarily done for two reasons. A psychoanalyst is writing about a particular clinical issue and needs case material to substantiate his argument. He inevitably selects vignettes—brief views of a particular moment in the analysis—to illustrate an idea. He is writing to members of his profession and the essay is often in technical language. This form of disclosure maintains confidence insofar as the psychoanalyst in effect is consulting with other colleagues, only in this case through a journal rather than in person.

But psychoanalysts also increasingly write for the lay public, in substantial part to convey the value of a psychoanalysis. When they do this they may write up an entire psychoanalysis as did Vamık Volkan (1984) in his moving account of a long analysis. Even with the patient's agreement, is this not a violation of the rule of confidentiality that we have maintained must be followed without exception? In what way does such disclosure differ from disclosure in a court? The response is obvious: disclosure of an analysis to a court or to a managed care provider reveals the identity of the patient; publication of aspects of an analysis secures that identity. In this area the psychoanalyst is not unlike a journalist. A journalist does reveal what a source has said to him but does not reveal who the source is. Moreover, psychoanalytic writing does not result in dire consequence to the patient or to anyone else. It falls within the domain of what we might call benign revelation. It is a form of disclosure aimed to advance the understanding of psychoanalysis, revealing something of what takes place. The reader will learn something about a patient's problems and psychoanalytical treatment, but will not learn who the patient is. Nonetheless, there are important guidelines to consider along the spectrum of psychoanalytic publications.

Provided that the patient is not a fellow mental health professional or a person at all likely to read the specialized psychoanalytic journals, it is our view that the psychoanalyst can proceed to publish selected vignettes from his clinical work with a patient without the patient's permission. We assume, however, that the patient's physical description and other details are altered by disinforming, creating a disguise that will conceal any identifying characteristics. We think that even with publication in an obscure psychoanalytic journal, however, a psychoanalyst should ordinarily secure permission from a patient to publish, and should hand a copy of the intended extracts to the patient for vetting. We do appreciate, however, that certain essays might convey views of a patient that would be needlessly distressing for the patient to read and that are nonetheless germane to the development of psychoanalysis. A psychoanalyst might want to write an essay on those parts of a person that were psychopathic, for example, with material that the patient would find too overwhelming to read. Much of psychoanalytic technique is concerned with putting difficult observations into manageable form for a patient. A short essay might be too traumatic. Psychoanalysts have come to the view that it is important for deeper understanding of psychoanalysis to write about countertransference, about what is taking place within them in work with a particular patient or type of patient (such as the anorexic or bulimic, for example). Material from the countertransference might be made selectively and tactfully available to the patient during the analysis, but nothing like a full disclosure of one's ongoing range of feelings ever takes place. For a patient to read what was going on within the psychoanalyst's mind would in many instances be an exceedingly disturbing event. And yet it is essential for publication that this sort of disclosure be possible, which we imagine is best done without patient knowledge in an appropriate journal that does not give permission for future publication elsewhere, such as in an anthology, without the author's permission.

The rule of concealing any identifying characteristics must also, naturally, hold for wider publication. This would include over-the-counter journals like *Free Associations* or the *Nouvelle Revue de Psychanalyse* as well as trade publications. We believe that there are certain books printed by specialist psychoanalytic publishing houses, such as Jason Aronson Inc. or the Analytic Press, where psychoanalysts could write about a patient without the patient's knowledge or permission. Again, and this is a point that bears repetition, the patient cannot be identifiable in any way other than to the psychoanalyst himself. The psychoanalyst needs to be free to write about certain aspects of a person, or details of his countertransference with the patient, without disclosing them to the patient. Provided that the patient is not in the field and is not interested in reading psychoanalytical material, provided, that is, that the psychoanalyst thinks the patient would in all likelihood not come by such a writing, then on balance these safeguards are sufficient. Normally, a psychoanalyst would know if the patient has informed friends in the profession that he is in analysis with the particular clinician. If this has occurred, it is more likely that a patient's friend may for whatever reason bring to the patient's attention the psychoanalyst's publication. This is one of the reasons psychoanalysts believe it is important for patients to keep the identity of their psychoanalyst in confidence.

However, if a patient or former patient is likely to read his psychoanalyst's writing about the analysis, even though he or she is disguised and even though the material is limited to highly selected vignettes, the psychoanalyst should ordinarily gain the patient's prior permission. This is especially important if the psychoanalyst in question writes books that sell outside the strictly psychoanalytic world. Even if the patient's identity is secured, such publication is a potential psychic violation of the analysand. To ensure that all patients may discuss with their psychoanalysts what takes place within them, they must be assured that appropriate guidelines will be followed in the consideration of publication. Ultimately the clinician should use his judgment. Certainly there will be patients for whom it would be intrusive to read an essay on their treatment.

It is our view that confidentiality can be restored to the practice of psychoanalysis only if the changes we have outlined take place. The profession must refuse under all circumstances to hand over clinical notes to anyone outside it and to testify in court about work with any patient. This includes the disclosure of session notes to third-party providers until such time as those providers are managed by professional peers and can guarantee confidentiality. Psychotherapists who inappropriately disclose the contents of a patient's analysis and identify that patient have committed an unethical action and should be censured by the profession. (The same is true of those who contribute to a biographer's writing of a patient's life.) Psychoanalysts can devise clear codes of practice and means of redress for patients that deal effectively with any ethical violation by a psychoanalyst. The international associations of psychoanalysis can ensure that proper guidelines are established for the dispensation of deceased psychoanalysts' records and define terms for writing up material from a particular analysis.

We believe that degradation of the psychoanalytical situation would not have occurred to the same extent if the public had a greater understanding of what psychoanalysis is and how it must function. To a considerable degree, the passivity of the psychoanalytic profession, in particular of its professional organizations, is largely to blame for the failure to respond adequately to a public misconception that led to legislative and regulatory actions that have unintentionally but seriously harmed psychoanalysis.

Indeed it is the curious lassitude on the part of psychoanalysts toward crucial features of their own profession that in our view explains why similar deteriorations in privilege are taking place in other countries. Reviewing the differences among countries regarding the protection of confidentiality is beyond the scope of our study. Many countries, however, have thus far refused to allow the sort of destruction of privilege we have outlined (see, for example, Mendelson and Mendelson [1991].)

In Sweden the Act on Secrecy (1980) states that privilege "shall not hinder" conveying information to a prosecutor or the police, if it is the clinician's view that he should inform the authorities of criminal intent or accomplishment on the part of a patient. This law ostensibly protects the clinician from prosecution by such a patient. However, in combination with several other Swedish Acts of Parliament—the Act on Obligation (1994), the Act on Supervision of Health and Medical Personnel (1980), and the Act on Patients' Case-Books (1985)—the law now operates as a conduit for mandatory reporting of certain crimes that would be punishable by two or more years of imprisonment. The Swedish system is complex and different mental health practitioners are under different obligations. A psychotherapist working for a social service agency is required to report certain confidences to the authorities, while a psychotherapist working privately is *less* obliged. The failure of the psychotherapy and psychoanalysis professions in Sweden to define their right to privilege has no doubt contributed to what amounts to considerable confusion in the present laws.

The British Association of Psychotherapists (BAP) (1994), a highly prestigious training association, illustrates in a recent publication how the profession can shirk its responsibility to preserve confidence by transferring the burden to another profession.

Members have asked what they should do when solicitors seek their opinions on patients, or when clinical notes are asked for. Our advice is that members should speak to their own solicitors in the first instance, and to say that any opinion a psychotherapist may have would not be helpful to the conduct of a case in court, on the grounds that psychotherapists are not usually in possession of actual contestable information, and that any opinion proffered could very easily be challenged by the other party. [p. 35]

While it is true—and we have argued—that much of what psychotherapists hear from their patients is provisional and ambiguous, there are occasions, as we know from litigation in the United States, when a clinician is informed of incontestable information, and his testimony in court would be decisive. The advice avoids the essential point: clinical notes contain confidential information and are therefore privileged. By asking lawyers to define clinical ethics, the BAP unwittingly abdicates its responsibility for the profession of psychotherapy.

The American Psychoanalytic Association, the International Psychoanalytical Association, and the International Federation of Psychoanalytic Societies, important organizations entrusted with the operations of psychoanalysis, are nonetheless run by rotating part-timers who, although well intentioned, are not up to the tasks of protecting and promoting psychoanalysis in the modern world.

Full-time professional staff will have to be sought from outside the profession to operate these organizations in a more coherent and productive way. The advice passed on to its members from the BAP reflects the fact that the officers of this organization have neither the time nor the expertise to define and defend analytical confidentiality.

It cannot be assumed, furthermore, that even an association dedicated to the preservation and promotion of psychoanalysis such as the American Psychoanalytic Association will ultimately fulfill such a trust. The overwhelming number of psychoanalysts in the association are trained in psychiatry. Many practitioners willingly cooperate with regulatory bodies that divest psychoanalysis of important rights; others sit on the boards of insurance companies connected to a managed care system that erodes the integrity of psychoanalytic practice, or have been indirectly subsidized in one way or another by the pharmaceutical industry. Quite possibly, therefore, there is an unwitting if not unconscious conflict of interest between their discipline of origin and their subsequent decision to become psychoanalysts. Can they move beyond those compromises accepted by their parent profession?[7]

---

7. Readers are referred to Peter Breggin's (1991) book *Toxic Psychiatry*, especially Chapter 15, "Psychiatry and the Psycho-Pharmaceutical Complex" for a disquieting analysis of the links between drug companies and the profession of psychiatry. Breggin illustrates how the pharmaceutical industry is

Many of these psychiatrist-psychoanalysts are
aware of the often profound conflict of interests
that prevail in the upper echelons of the American
Psychiatric Association, some of whose leading officials have been paid consultants to leading pharmaceutical corporations, where major drug companies have substantially underwritten the costs of
the association's national conventions, and where
its major journals and publications derive revenue
essential to their survival from paid advertisements
from those companies that have vested interests in
putting medication before psychotherapy and psychoanalysis (Breggin 1991). Even though many of
them would disown these links, it is hard not to conclude that the psychiatrist-psychoanalyst who has
been in a unique position to defend psychoanalysis and distinguish it from psychiatry has substantially failed to do so. Nowhere is this more evident
than in the failure to evaluate critically the impact
of forensic psychiatry on the clinical standards offered to the patient by the profession. It seems unlikely, therefore, that simple lassitude on the part
of the American Psychoanalytic Association can
explain the failure to take action against these deep

---

an important part of the psychiatrist's training, professional
development, and ultimately, clinical practice. And although
his book reads at times like fright fiction, and one must regard many of his claims as just the beginning of a deeper investigation into the situation, it is nonetheless startling that
it has taken so long for such a book to be written.

encroachments on psychoanalytic privilege. The psychiatrist-psychoanalyst comes from a brotherhood deeply invested in participation with state- and corporate-sponsored regulation. If and when that alliance conflicts with the principles of psychoanalysis, psychoanalysis loses.

Between 1974 and 1981, the American did take some significant steps to protect confidentiality through the work of its Joint (with the American Psychiatric Association) Ad Hoc Committee on Confidentiality (JAHCC, later JCC). These steps included the promulgation of a consent form for the disclosure of information to insurers that automatically expired after one year, publication of a model statute that protected an analyst's personal notes from disclosure, the development of guidelines for members to be followed where a search warrant was used to seize records, and the submission of *amicus curiae* briefs (sometimes by member Institutes) in several cases, including *Tarasoff*, where confidentiality was an issue. However, since 1989, the files of the committee reflect a certain demoralization about the issue, with information about new and recurring threats to confidentiality but no references to any concrete action by the Association. This issue is, however, of urgent interest to Dr. Judith Schachter, President of the American, and we can hope certain definitive action is forthcoming.

Psychoanalysis benefits from important contributions to the understanding of certain organic processes operating in the psychic field brought to it from its medical practitioners. Unfortunately, the same practitioners also bring with them a tradition of reciprocity between their profession and the psychopharmaceutical–managed care industry, which, it need be repeated, has become openly and vigorously opposed to the value of psychotherapy and psychoanalysis. We believe this partnership is of no meaningful consequence to the vast number of practicing psychoanalysts within the association who would rightly claim that they are hardly persuaded to abandon the psychoanalytic perspective by drug advertisements. However, we take this developing conflict of interest to be a good example— we could instead focus on social work or psychology or one of the humanities, where other conflicts of interest reside—and an occasion to reiterate that psychoanalysis must become an independent profession. The failures of psychoanalysis to critically deconstruct conflicts of interest residing in the dual role—social worker-psychoanalyst, psychologist-psychoanalyst, psychiatrist-psychoanalyst—simply reflects, in our view, the range and degree of a conflict that can ironically enough flourish precisely because the psychoanalysts who emerge from these traditions cease to have any real interest in the profession of origins. We do not argue that these psychoanalysts actually benefit from alliances with the regulatory agencies or managed care institutions— only a very few really do—but that their inattention to these matters resulted in power vacuums in the disciplines of origin that were subsequently filled by individuals whose conflicts of interest are substantial and destructive.

It is time now to redress this situation and to allow psychoanalysis to defend itself free of debilitating conflicts of interest. If the psychoanalytic organizations thus far entrusted with moral and political effectiveness are to ultimately earn the positive regard of those practicing psychoanalysis, and those who would look upon it as a future career, they will have to look critically at their failures and undertake appropriate reorganizations. We know very well that the great majority of practicing psychoanalysts—of whatever discipline of origin—are deeply devoted to their work and to psychoanalysis. It is to these colleagues and others that we now turn. Having charted a worrying period in psychoanalytic history, we hope we have brought the issues into sharper focus and also indicated clear pathways to change.

REFERENCES

Alfaro, J. (1985). *Impediments to mandated reporting of suspected child abuse and neglect in New York City.* Paper presented at the Seventh National Conference on Child Abuse and Neglect, Chicago, IL.

American Psychiatric Association. (1987). *Guidelines on Confidentiality.* Washington, DC: APA.

———— (1989). *Paul Appelbaum on Law and Psychiatry.* Washington, DC: APA (H & CP Service).

———— (1993a). *Practice Guidelines for Major Depression Disorder in Adults.* Washington, DC: APA.

———— (1993b). *The Principle of Medical Ethics.* Washington, DC: APA.

———— (1993c). *Opinion of the Ethics Committee on the Principles of Medical Ethics.* Washington, DC: APA.

———(1994). *Diagnostic and Statistical Manual of Mental Disorders*, 4th ed. Washington, DC: APA.

Berlin, F. S., Malin, H. M., and Dean, S. (1991). Effects of statutes requiring psychiatrists to report suspected sexual abuse of children. *American Journal of Psychiatry* 148(4):449–453.

Bernstein, R. (1994). Lawyer risks jail to protect client information. *The New York Times*, December 23, p. A14.

Black, D., Wolkind, S., and Hendriks, J. H., eds. (1989). *Child Psychiatry and the Law*. London: Royal College of Psychiatry.

Bollas, C. (1987). *The Shadow of the Object*. New York: Columbia University Press.

Breggin, P. (1991). *Toxic Psychiatry*. New York: St. Martin's Press.

British Association of Psychotherapists. (1994). *Newsletter* 21:35.

California Center for Health Statistics. (1974). Report on specialized child protective services for California. Legal files, unpublished.

Carvajal, D. (1995). Family photos or pornography? A father's bitter legal odyssey. *The New York Times*, January 30, p. 1.

Casement, P. (1985). *On Learning from the Patient*. London: Tavistock.

Cernusch, C. (1992). *Jackson Pollock: "Psychoanalytic" Drawings*. Durham, NC: Duke University Press.

Chafee, Z. (1943). Privileged communications: is justice served or obstructed by closing the doctor's mouth on the witness stand? *Yale Law Journal* 52:607.

Chekhov, A. *The Short Stories of Anton Chekhov*. (1932). Ed. R. N. Linscott. New York: Random House (Modern Library).

Chiswick, D. (1995). Dangerousness. In *Practical Forensic Psychiatry*, ed. D. Chiswick and R. Cope. London: Royal College of Psychiatrists-Gaskell.

Crimes Clog the Courts. (1992). *Oakland Tribune*, December 13, p. 1.

Eastman, N. L. G. (1987). Clinical Confidentiality: a contractual basis. *Issues in Criminological and Legal Psychology* 11:49–57.

Erikson, E. (1950). *Childhood and Society*. New York: W. W. Norton.

Frankenstein, A. (1977). Laying the Pollock case to rest. *Art News* 76:96.

Goldberg, D. (1992). Psychologist isn't immune for report. *San Francisco Daily Journal*, December 7, p. 1.

Goldstein, J., Freud, A., Solnit, A. J., and Goldstein, S. (1986). *In the Best Interests of the Child*. New York: Free Press.

Goldstein, R. L. (1990). New extension of the *Tarasoff* decision. *American Journal of Psychiatry* 147(9): 1250–1251.

Grunwald, M. (1995). A family's nightmare—false child-abuse charge. *San Francisco Chronicle*, January 30, p. A8.

Gur, B. (1992). *The Saturday Morning Murder*. New York: HarperCollins.

Hartigan, K. (1994). *The erosion of psychotherapists' autonomy by the insurance industry: who is responsible for therapeutic processes and outcomes*. Paper presented at the Illinois Psychological Association Convention, November 3.

Hartmann, H. (1958). *The Ego and the Problem of Adaptation*. New York: International Universities Press.

Haugaard, J. J., and Reppucci, N. D. (1988). *The Sexual Abuse of Children*. San Francisco and London: Jossey-Bass.

Hayman, A. (1965). Psychoanalyst subpoenaed. *Lancet*, October 16, pp. 785–786.

Henneberger, M. (1994). Managed care changing practice of psychotherapy. *New York Times*, October 9.

Jagim, R., et al. (1978). Mental health professionals' attitudes toward confidentiality, privilege and third-party disclosure. *Professional Psychology* 9:458–459.

Kalichman, S. C. (1993). *Mandated Reporting of Suspected Child Abuse: Ethics, Law and Policy*, Washington, DC: American Psychological Association.

Kalichman, S. C., and Craig, M. E. (1987). *Mental health professionals' attitudes and tendency to report*. Paper presented at the Second World Congress for Victimology, Orlando, FL.

Knapp, S., and VendeCreek, L. (1987). *Privileged Communications in the Mental Health Professions*, New York: Van Nostrand Reinhold.

McDougall, J. (1980). *Plea for a Measure of Abnormality*. New York: International Universities Press.

Mendelson, D., and Mendelson, G. (1991). Tarasoff down under: the psychiatrist's duty to warn in Australia. *Journal of Psychiatry and Law* 19:33–61.

Middlebrook, D. W. (1991). *Anne Sexton: A Biography*. Boston: Houghton Mifflin.

Miller, I. J. (1994). *What Managed Care is Doing to Outpatient Mental Health*. Boulder, CO: Boulder Psychotherapists' Press.

Mrazek, P. J. (1983). Bibliography of books on child sexual abuse. *Child Abuse and Neglect* 7:247–249.

Paulsen, M., Parker, G., and Adelman, L. (1966). Child abuse reporting laws—some legislative history. *George Washington Law Review* 34:482.

Poynter, W. L. (1994). *The Preferred Provider's Handbook*. New York: Brunner/Mazel.

Renshaw, D. C. (1987). Evaluating suspected cases of child sexual abuse. *Psychiatric Annals* 17:262–270.

Slovenko, R. (1974). Psychotherapist-patient testimonial privilege: a picture of misguided hope. *Catholic University Law Review* 23:650.

Some therapy tapes can be used. (1992). *San Francisco Daily Journal*, August 28, p. 1.

Stephens, E. M. (1994). Managed (denial) care: do we have a legal remedy? *Academy Forum* (*American Academy of Psychoanalysis*) 38(4):16–17.

Tester, M. A. (1986). *The Scott County sexual abuse cases: a closer look at what went wrong*. Unpublished manuscript, Department of Psychology, University of Virginia.

Volkan, V. (1984). *What Do You Get When You Cross a Dandelion with a Rose?*, New York: Jason Aronson.

Walker, L. E., Alpert, J., Harris, E., and Koocher, G. (1989). *Report to the APA Board of Directors from the Ad Hoc Committee on Child Abuse Policy*. Washington, DC: American Psychological Association.

Walls, G. B. (1994). *Biological determinism, managed care and the new political right*. Paper presented at the Annual Meeting of the Illinois Psychological Association, November 4.

Weisberg, D. K. (1984). The discovery of sexual abuse: experts' role in legal policy formulation. *University of California–Davis Law Review* 18:1–57.

Wright, L. (1994). *Remembering Satan*. New York: Knopf.

INDEX